May Good things follow You!

Rejection

Samira

Rejection

an agent of
SUCCESS

A Story of Trial and Triumph

SAMIRA OTUNG

Matador
Unit E2 Airfield Business Park,
Harrison Road, Market Harborough,
Leicestershire. LE16 7UL
Tel: 0116 2792299
Email: books@troubador.co.uk
Web: www.troubador.co.uk/matador
Twitter: @matadorbooks

ISBN 978 1800464 803

British Library Cataloguing in Publication Data.
A catalogue record for this book is available from the British Library.

Printed and bound in Great Britain by 4edge Limited
Typeset in 11pt Minion Pro by Troubador Publishing Ltd, Leicester, UK

Matador is an imprint of Troubador Publishing Ltd

To the One who never sleeps nor slumbers, always watching over me. To all those who have prayed for me, supported me through my trying times.

To my beautiful Princess for being so brave and understanding.

Acknowledgements

Special thanks to God for giving me the courage to persevere with this book.

Thanks to Bishop Dag Heward Mills, for being a great role model to me and for believing that people like me can also do the work of the ministry (the beautiful job!).

Thanks to my husband, extended family and friends.

Finally, I am grateful for my enemies as God will always prepare a table before me in their presence!

Contents

Preface

You hold in your hands the unfolding story and testimony of how I went through some dark times of rejection in my life. This book seeks to encourage you as the reader, with the good news that it does not matter who you are, where you are and what you have done; what really matters is who you are destined to be and you are a loved by God.

In the course of writing the book, I have found myself debating on just how much detail of my experience I should share, what to include or leave out, who to mention and who to leave out. This is because my testimony involves other people and I was not sure if they were ready to 'own' their part of my story. I also wanted to be sure of my motive for sharing some very personal details of my life. Nevertheless, I am fully persuaded that writing this book is in obedience to my Heavenly Father, on His instruction to testify of the things He has taught me through troubles.

One day, I was at an all-night prayer meeting when God gave me some instructions. He said I should write 'My testimony', i.e., experiences of major events in my life that will help others. I wondered if I heard right and delayed for a while but later received further confirmation when God laid out to me what should be shared and how to go about it.

The things we go through are for us to 'discover' ourselves and learn. They are also for the benefit and blessing of others. Take Apostle Peter for example,

"… the Lord said, 'Simon, Simon! Indeed, Satan has asked for you, that he may sift you as wheat. But I have prayed for you, that your faith should not fail; **and when you have returned to Me, strengthen your brethren.**'"

(Luke 22:31-32 emphasis added)

What Jesus is saying in a nutshell is, Peter would have been through much worse if he was not prayed for; Therefore, he should hold on to his faith, not lose hope and once he recovers from the temptation, he should also encourage others. Peter did just that. He rose above the guilt and shame he must have experienced for betraying Jesus and he went on to accomplish many great miracles. The Book of Acts records that he boldly testified of his experience with Jesus. (2:14-41)

Like Peter, most of us have had moments in our lives we are not proud of but we must learn to rise above these experiences in order to become victorious. It is so wonderful to have a relationship with Jesus, especially as He makes up for all our imperfections, thereby enabling us to experience true peace and freedom. Peter's testimony touched many people's hearts so much so that about three thousand people came to know and follow Jesus in one day.

Jesus wants to turn our mess into a message of hope for others, our tests into testimonies, our trials into triumphs, and use our challenges as a pre-requisite for change.

I believe God will use this book to inspire you to overcome every form of rejection, pain, hurt and be a victor. Remember your story is also unfolding and in the fullness of time, you will also be a great help and blessing to others. As Spurgeon stated,

> "A dead calm is our enemy; a storm may prove our helper. Controversy may arouse thought, and through thought may come the Divine change."
>
> *Charles Spurgeon (1834-1892)*

God in His infinite mercy, will keep you and protect you as you let Him into your heart. I pray that you will receive strength and grace to overcome rejection, in Jesus' Name! Amen. God Bless you.

Samira Otung

Chapter 1

Familiar Foe

'He was despised and rejected by mankind, a man of
suffering, and familiar with pain. Like one from whom
people hide their faces he was despised, and we held
him in low esteem.'

[Isaiah 53:3]

Rejection is a common emotion we all face frequently.
It is a familiar foe. In this chapter I will share my
experiences of rejection. Ultimately, the underlying
question is – how can we process and convert the rejection
we face into a force or a springboard, which can be used to
propel us into ultimate success in life. How can you avoid
being bitter when someone you trust has betrayed you?

Thinking about the good, which may come from
being rejected is the last thing on anyone's mind at the
point of rejection. However, I have come to understand it
is sometimes best to 'brace yourself' for rejection because

it will most certainly come. Bracing yourself for rejection does not necessarily make the blow feel any softer, it just makes it bearable if handled correctly. It should eventually yield a better character in us.

The different forms and sources of rejection can lead to different mental and emotional effects. It is the act of pushing someone or something away. It can even be an act of refusing to acknowledge or validate someone or something. Rejection might be experienced on a large scale or in small ways in everyday life. This could be rejection from family, friends, and relationships or in a marriage.

I have, on many occasions been rejected. I felt rejected by my own father as a child, so never really got to know him. I only knew him to be some rich Muslim man with other wives and children. I had no way of knowing if he cared for me, as I only heard stories of him from my mum and they were not always pleasant. Curiosity and loneliness would always force me to wonder what it would be like to have a relationship with my father.

In 2011, I decided to search for my father on Facebook. I found someone with the same last name, I suspected we could be related and requested for friendship. It turned out the person was indeed my cousin. He connected me to my father. How happy I was! How I felt hearing his voice, was indescribable. He told me he had been looking for me and was sorry for not looking hard enough. He had converted from Islam to Christianity and his pastor had advised him to look for me. He told me how happy he was to speak with me and he could now die a happy man.

I was happy yet cautious, as if it was too good to be true. I had a warm feeling of 'belonging'. I had a father, my own biological father. I must have spoken to him either once or twice. However, before I could fully decipher and digest my feelings, I received a phone call informing me he had died of a stroke – just two weeks after finding him on Facebook. I was heartbroken. The wounds of rejection were again open, with a crushing sense of grief and loss. Yet again, I was left feeling un-loved and not belonging to anyone or anywhere; consequently, a lot of anger and bitterness built up inside of me. Though I was very independent, I found myself relying heavily on people for emotional support but then it would lead to further rejection – the cycle continued.

My stepfather taught me some good things (i.e., how to do certain chores/cooking etc.), which I will always be grateful for. However, in the cause of trying to 'win' my mothers' complete attention he would manipulate situations i.e., he would say one thing when my mum was around and another thing when she is not there to make me look bad. So, it's my words against his in a bid to win my mother's approval. This made me feel rejected and unwanted, like the 'black sheep' of the family. It got so bad at one point that I considered taking my own life. I recall seeking help from my secondary school guidance counsellor.

Dear reader, please do not hesitate to get help no matter how insignificant your mental struggles may seem.

There was a point in my life where it felt like all hell broke loose… My marriage was heading for divorce; I was facing a crisis at church; I lost a close family friend who was like a sister to me to kidney failure; I had to undergo surgery to remove nodules from my vocal chords. My job was under threat, I was under financial, physical, emotional and spiritual strain.

I felt my world crumbling all around me. Suicide looked like an easy way out. The thoughts would come as a suggestion of a 'simple solution'. All I could do was muster up some courage to cry to God for help. Though He seemed so far, I could still feel Him near, telling me to hold on and not give in to those thoughts. I also overcame the urge to 'self-destruct' by focusing my mind on what 'could be' rather than 'what is'. I had to remind myself of the 'good things' no matter how small. I would conclude that it's actually not that bad after all, it really could have been worse.

Although rejection seemed to be an ever-present familiar foe in my life, I thank God I can forgive those who rejected me. I can only pray that others can also forgive me. I admit it is not an easy feat and each day presents yet another occasion for someone to reject me or me to reject someone either knowingly or unknowingly. God has blessed me with the grace to let go and He has turned everything around for my good. I pray for you today as you read these words, for the healing power of God to wash over you. You shall see the end of this painful period if only you do not give up!

Although most people can easily identify with the feeling of being rejected, not many people will readily admit, they too have rejected others. It is sometimes necessary to reject some people or some things. The key is how the rejection is done and how sensitive you are to the one being rejected. The aim must be "...*speaking the truth in love...*" so you "*may grow up in all things into Him who is the head – Christ.*" (Ephesians 4:15)

The most 'interesting' part of feeling rejected is that it sneaks up on you. You cannot control others' perception of you and you will always feel their rejection is undeserved.

People tend to develop rejection-handling mechanisms such as counter-rejection, where you reject others; self-blame; various forms of emotional defence mechanisms, which includes the 'I don't care/it doesn't bother me' attitude.

Whichever way you choose to deal with rejection, it is essential to understand, things happen for a reason, so it's good to always look at the overall picture.

Rejection can come in different forms: emotional, physical, psychological, financial, social, spiritual, and oddly enough – even biological. Whilst emotion has to do with feelings, psychology relates to a person's mental state; a mentally unstable person may then go on to have an emotional imbalance.

Emotional Rejection

It is safe to say, all forms of rejection will most likely have an element of emotion in it. Rejection is a type of feeling you experience when a need is not met. It may be a disappointment; but when a person has an emotional need such as a need for love or affection but does not receive it, this can have a devastating impact their emotional and mental wellbeing. A child can feel emotionally rejected by their parents even though the parent are physically. Not getting a deserved compliment and acknowledgement from a loved one can make a person feel emotionally rejected. A romantic gesture or advances not returned or acknowledged, may result in emotional rejection.

On many occasions I have felt emotionally rejected when circumstances forced me to remember that I have lost my biological father. Jesus felt emotionally rejected by

His Heavenly Father during His crucifixion when He cried out with a loud voice, saying, *"Eloi, Eloi, lama sabachthani?" which is translated, "My God, My God, why have You forsaken Me?"* (Mark 15:34)

Physical Rejection

An example of this is where individuals have a physical ailment, which makes people not want to physically associate with them. Wives and husbands may also feel physically rejected by their spouses when they refuse to have sex with them or cheat on them because of shortcomings in their physique/sensuality.

In my earlier years, I attended a boarding school in Nigeria. For some reason I felt it 'cool' to experiment with a stick to see if I could put it through the right ear, to come out of the left ear! Obviously, that did not work and it caused a massive damage to my ear drum to this day.

During that time, I started getting a mucus-like substance from my right ear. This would constantly pour out of my ear, smelly and thick. I had to carry cotton wool wherever I went to clean my ears. It was really embarrassing. People would point at me and some would recoil in disgust. I was physically rejected. This carried on into my teenage years. It impacted my self-confidence. I lived with my grandmother at the time, and she took me to visit an 'herbal doctor'. Nothing worked! When I returned to the city, someone suggested, we pour 'red and yellow' capsules down the infected ear – and it worked!

This state of physical rejection transposed over the years to other situations. The most painful were my husband's frequent infidelities because I was not 'sensual enough' according to him, and my previous employers' rejection of me because 'my face' simply did not fit the organisation.

There are no doubt, many like me who have been physically rejected and forsaken because of how they look, or who they are. You are not alone. We learn from scriptures that Joseph was physically rejected by his brothers. He was sold into slavery.

> "So it came to pass, when Joseph had come to his brothers, that they stripped Joseph of his tunic, the tunic of many colours that was on him. Then they took him and cast him into a pit. And the pit was empty; there was no water in it ... Then Midianite traders passed by: so, the brothers pulled Joseph up and lifted him out of the pit, and sold him to the Ishmaelites for twenty shekels of silver. And they took Joseph to Egypt."
>
> *(Genesis 37:23-28)*

Another person who was physically rejected but seldom mentioned is Mephibosheth, son of Jonathan, grandson of King Saul.

> "So, David said to him, 'Do not fear, for I will surely show you kindness for Jonathan your father's sake, and will restore to you all the land of Saul your grandfather; and you shall eat bread at my table continually.' Then he bowed himself, and said, 'What is your servant, that you should look upon such a dead dog as I?'"
>
> *(2 Samuel 9:7-8)*

You see – this grandson of Saul was lame and could not walk, and so he had been rejected by his extended family. No one remembered him, no one honoured him, not even for his father or grandfather's sake. He was forgotten and rejected. Thank God for people like King David who remembered him and showed him kindness. May you also be remembered in Jesus' Name!

Psychological Rejection

This can be experienced because of negative words or insinuations. Lies told against you constantly or your perception of someone's behaviour towards you can lead to psychological rejection. Emotional blackmail has some psychological effects on the intended recipient. Just as 'the mind can play tricks on you', so can words. Actions or lack thereof can play tricks on your mind. Words or actions of people can make you feel rejected even if it was not intended to have that effect. In your mind you may feel psychologically rejected but it is possible the rejection is not real.

Everyone experiences this but again, if not carefully addressed, it can leave a lasting impression or rejection. I remember my four-year-old daughter crying one day. I asked why she was crying and she said "Daddy doesn't want me". I was taken aback that she would interpret her dad's correction for bad behaviour to mean she was unloved and rejected. Immediately I understood just how rejection can become established in our lives from an early age. I used the opportunity to educate her that her Daddy loves and wants her but wants her to be good so being told off is not the same as being unwanted. Psychologically, many people feel rejected when in fact it is far from the truth.

Financial Rejection

This is a rejection of wealth. There are some people who associate having money with being a bad person. There are others who feel accumulating wealth is not something to strive for but rather something to avoid. In the extreme, those feelings can develop into a serious money disorder, which financial therapists[2] call 'financial rejection'. So, you can be rejected when you try to use your wealth for good because someone thinks you have ulterior motives and as such they reject you and your money.

It could also mean; people reject you because of your lack of money. It is a fact that *"Wealth makes many friends, But the poor is separated from his friend."* (Proverbs 19:4)

Social Rejection

This type of rejection is fast becoming a major cause for concern in this century. It can come from friends whether real or cyber. We are in the age of instant gratification and validation. The need to be liked, noticed, approved of and praised, has greatly increased and so these social expectations lead to constant exposure to rejection. It is understandable to feel sad when your friends or family comment negatively on a photo or do not approve of your efforts. The problem with this era is that nowadays a person can feel utterly rejected by the actions or comments of a total stranger on the internet.

The packaging of one's image purposely and solely for the approval and validation of others is a recipe for rejection. Companies and Brands now pay people to be social influencers, therefore adding to the pressure and need to be 'liked' and 'followed'. The more people like you, the more you get paid. The approval or disapproval of subscribers or followers/friends has a huge influence on the social influencers themselves. You are influenced by the people you influence. How ironic! There are many who experience depression and anxiety as a result of this type of rejection.

In America, case studies were conducted of 15 school shootings between 1995 and 2001 to examine the possible role of social rejection in school violence. The study found that acute or chronic rejection such as in the form of ostracism, bullying, and/or romantic rejection was present in all but two of the incidents. [3]

Dear reader, please do not give anyone the power to control your emotions in such a way. I pray you receive freedom from such strongholds, in Jesus' Name!

Biological rejection

In layman's terms, this is when your body actively rejects foreign elements introduced into your system. The body can reject elements introduced into the body regardless of whether it is good for the body or not.

We are born with biological defence systems that are to block any foreign elements. However, there are also other biological receptors designed to help recognise or process these 'foreign elements' to either say it's 'ok' or 'not ok' to accept the introduced elements. A problem can occur if the body then rejects something, which could be of help to it. For example, a patient with kidney failure may die because the body keeps rejecting the donor kidney (foreign element) transplanted to it.

Spiritual Rejection

This type of rejection is perhaps less acknowledged. Even in church circles, many are very oblivious to the ever-opportunistic spirit of rejection. I say it is an opportunistic spirit because it seizes every opportunity to sustain the feelings of rejection. Later on, we see the ultimate aim of the spirit of rejection is for its carrier to self-destruct. When you are spiritually rejected, you feel perhaps God has rejected you. You may well feel alone in your school, family, work, church, social circle and so on; but to feel utterly alone in the world and universe is intense, and the effects are far-reaching. This type of rejection is the one we cannot see but works to bring all the other above forms of rejection to fruition, because any rejection in the physical results from a corresponding spiritual power behind it.

It explains the complicated need to continually expose ourselves to the people or environment that is not helpful to us. It explains the burden to impress incessantly. This spirit of rejection works hand in hand with fear – the fear of being alone, not liked, not approved of, of making mistakes and dying, just to illustrate some examples.

Rejection is a respecter of no one. Everyone and anyone can feel rejected at any time, for any reason and for however long.

Stages of Rejection

The stages of rejection[4] can be better explained through the medical terms used in the context of the body rejecting an organ transplant.

- Stage 1: Hyper-acute

  This type of rejection is seen when a recipient is given the wrong type of blood, for example, when a person is given type A blood when he or she is type B. Hyper-acute rejection occurs a few minutes after the body recognises that the antigens are completely unmatched. The tissue must be removed right away so the recipient does not die.

  In a social context, you can experience rejection as soon as you enter a new environment, or you find yourself in situation that is unfamiliar to you. It can happen in the early stage where perhaps you have never met certain people before, but you can sense they do not want you around and you sense the rejection. Therefore, to use colloquialism, a hyper-acute rejection is experienced when a person is exposed to 'bad blood' when he or she is least expecting it. The term is used broadly to mean 'anything not good for you' or 'something/someone you are adverse to'.

- Stage 2: Acute rejection

  This may occur any time from the first week after the transplant to 3 months afterwards. All recipients have some amount of acute rejection.

In a social context, after you are slightly settled into a new environment or new situation, you begin to react to what you think are people's perception of you. You start to mark and avoid those who you feel are rejecting you. The feeling and reality of rejection starts to set in a few weeks or months after a spouse leaves the marriage for another person or when your employers inform you of your replacement. Indeed, all those who experience such adverse behaviour will feel some amount of acute rejection.

- Stage 3: Chronic rejection
  Chronic rejection can take place over many years. The body's constant immune response against the new organ slowly damages the transplanted tissues or organ.

  In a social context, if rejection is not dealt with effectively at the early stages, it becomes a chronic situation. One major rejection such as a father walking away from his children, or a husband leaving his wife for another, can have a lasting effect on a person's life. It may also be a series of rejections that could then lead to a person feeling broken for life. For example, a child bullied at school may then experience rejection at work leading to low confidence and low self-worth in a relationship where they further experience rejection.

A series of rejections taking place over the years can make a heart hardened, defensive, broken and destructive if not properly addressed and hopefully healed.

Rejection perhaps is the step-brother to betrayal in the level of hurt. When rejected, your expectation of how you should be received or how a situation should pan out is betrayed. You feel it strongly against your person when someone does not want what you offer or the person you are.

Therefore, it is a painful experience, and most will agree the pain of rejection can be felt physically leading to acute pain.

When a group of scientists[5] placed people in functional MRI machines and asked them to recall a recent rejection, they discovered something interesting. They discovered the same areas of our brain become activated when we experience rejection as when we experience physical pain.

This explains why even, what is deemed to be a 'small' rejection, can hurt more than we think it should, because it produces literal (albeit, emotional) pain.

Many would argue, they are accustomed to rejection, insisting they do not care or they are not affected by it and perhaps rightly so. However, denial is not a good and lasting defence to dealing with the seed of rejection planted in our hearts. It is better to acknowledge it hurts, and admit you would prefer not to be in that situation. Accept, people are entitled to their opinion of you and there will always be situations beyond your control.

There is medicine for physical pain, either to remove the pain completely or to endure the pain 'till the wounds heal'. However, there is no medical response as such for a wounded and rejected soul. This is the reason why many end up with all sorts of personality disorders, anxiety, self-hate, people hate, suicide, malice, even resorting to murder

– all because the pain of rejection cannot be dealt with by mere medicine.

Endnotes

1: My Bishop and favourite preacher Dag Heward Mills has a book titled *'Those Who Leave You'*, the book addresses the phenomenon of people's forgeul and ungrateful natures. I recommend you get his '7 Series' on loyalty and disloyalty.

2: www.financaltherapyassociaon.org
(accessed March 25, 2019).

3: www.onlinelibrary.wiley.com/doi/full/10.1002/ab.10061
(accessed March 25, 2019).

4: www.medlineplus.gov/ency/arcle/000815.htm
(accessed March 26, 2019).

5: www.pnas.org/content/pnas/108/15/6270.full.pdf
(accessed April 17, 2019).

Chapter 2

Effects of Rejection

There is always a cause and effect in many situations we face. Ishikawa diagrams are business analysis tool used to identify the causes and effects of problems. It is futile to try using a diagram to understand what causes people to have failed relationships or commitment issues and the effects they have on their decision-making processes. Can we ever explain, for example, why a child grows up to become a serial killer or a spouse beater; why people become bitter and insecure about their appearance; or why a person just feels constantly depressed and suicidal, feeling they do not belong in the world anymore? With or without the diagrams, you will see, you can no longer neglect the effect rejection of any kind, has on you. Even if you are successful in life, you may still relive the pain of rejection, when others said you were not good enough.

I remember feeling rejected when someone told me I was aggressive and unladylike. That day I had met someone

I look up to and admire. In my excitement I must have appeared 'too eager' or perhaps did not pay much attention to those around. Suddenly someone around us just looked at me with disgust and said, *"you are too aggressive, try to be ladylike"*. Whilst I appreciate that this may have been given as advice, the way in which it was said and the environment we were in, literally caused me to shut down that evening. My well-meaning intentions had been rejected and misconstrued. I must admit I was hurt at the time and, though I am well over the situation and learnt from it, I always remember the scar whenever I tell the story to others.

Physical and Mental Effects of Rejection

There was a study[1] conducted, which perhaps best explains the physical effects of rejection.

The Purpose of the Study

The experiments were meant to help scientists work with people who 'feel' rejected and teach them how to respond appropriately.

Study Group

124 healthy young adults were recruited by scientists at UCLA to participate in a lab-based test aimed at determining whether social stress such as rejection, causes inflammation, which can have detrimental effects on mental and physical health.

The idea was that they would be playing a 'game' with other 'people'. Unbeknown to them, the game was fictional and they were playing with 'imaginary' people. In effect these participating young adults were put through stressful tests designed to make them feel rejected.

These volunteers were made to feel as if they were messing up the game and the 'imaginary' people had suddenly stopped playing without reason.

The same participants took part in a computerised ball-tossing game while lying in a functional magnetic resonance imaging machine, programmed to light up brain regions that showed stress.

What did they find?

Brain regions associated with fear, stress, and rejection lit up. People who showed the greatest neural responses to being excluded during 'the game' also had shown the greatest increase in inflammatory activity. So those individuals who were most sensitive to social rejection, showed the greatest biological responses to that acute stressor of public speaking.

The study showed not surprisingly, that the inflammatory biological markers in oral fluids increased dramatically after the stressful tests.

In other words, we are likely to show signs of stress and rejection when we feel someone no longer wants to be our friend or we are being 'left out' of something others have been included in.

Scientists confirm, rejection triggers responses in the body that can increase a person's risk for illnesses such as asthma, arthritis, cardiovascular disease and depression.

In another study, testing the hypothesis that rejection mimics physical pain, researchers gave some volunteers acetaminophen (Tylenol – a strong painkiller) before asking them to recall a painful experience of rejection. The people who received Tylenol reported significantly less emotional pain than participants who took a placebo – sugar pill. Psychologists assume, the reason for the strong link between rejection and physical pain is that Tylenol reduces the emotional pain caused by rejection.

Thanks to science, should we consider taking some strong pain killers to numb the pain of rejection? I imagine many people resort to other recreational drugs and beverages to give 'high spirits' in the wake of rejection. However as mentioned before and as many will find, no amount of substance can quite deal with the pain of rejection. Even if there is no more pain associated with the rejection, the scar left behind reminds you of your ordeal.

Emotional Effects of Rejection

Emotions can be quite deceptive at times. Our emotions are what make us human, and they can be used as a weapon or a defence. Emotions, if not controlled or cultivated effectively can cause a lot of damage. Any human who claims to be unemotional is either in denial or has mastered the art of disguise and deception. Even Hollywood's Iron Man, who supposedly has no 'fleshy' heart still has emotions.

Rejection is of course one of many emotions one will go through in a lifetime, perhaps more often than other types of unpleasant emotions. Many researchers suggest, perhaps the reason why rejection hurts more is because it served a vital function in our evolutionary past (Not to be confused with Darwin's Theory of Evolution). It is said, in our hunter/gatherer past, being disliked/excluded/ alienated from our tribes was similar to a death sentence; this is because we were unlikely to cope on our own for a long time.

Evolutionary psychologists assume the brain developed an innate warning system to alert us when we were at risk for exclusion/shunning. The brain thinks it's so important to get our attention quickly, to correct our behaviour in order to remain in the tribe. It was concluded, perhaps this explains why many have the fear of being alone, fear of not being accepted by the community, even by the cyber community on social media and the fear of not being liked or validated.

Personally, I am of the mind that we must have the confidence to be alone and comfortable in our own skin, be happy with ourselves and be content with who we are as individuals. However contrary to many 'self-loving mantras' out there, I am also of the school of thought, we are not created to be lone beings, *"It is not good for man to be alone."* (Genesis 2:18) We are interdependent and co-dependent on fellow humans. We need one another.

Just as a tree cannot make a forest on its own, a person is dependent on another person to become a 'people'. There may be many theories and ideologies out there, which seem to suggest, one human being can survive on a whole planet alone. Whilst these theories can make a good movie, in reality we cannot overlook the fact that other people's actions, past and present, have a part to play in our lives.

Wanting to be in isolation and away from other humans is a 'learned behaviour'. Although some prefer their own company more than the company of others, it might just be their temperament. However, to actively want to be left alone, 'in the dark', with no human contact, is not natural and in many cases, it is driven by rejection and life's unpleasant experiences.

There is a reason why God built in us, the need for one another. It may be in order to cultivate love, unity and humility. Although one may argue, this need for one another has been perverted and thwarted by the enemy thus causing us to become rather selfish and destructive, there's no denying that built within us is the need to belong, to feel a part of something 'happening'. Therefore, when we are rejected, it de-stabilises our sense of belonging. It is this disconnection and helplessness, which heightens our emotional pain.

A report on Youth Violence[2] stated: rejection was a greater risk for adolescent violence than drugs, poverty, or gang membership. This is because rejection creates surges of anger and aggression. Many more studies have demonstrated, even mild rejections lead people to take out their aggression on innocent bystanders. Shootings at schools, restaurants, and concerts in the USA are becoming a common outlet for people who have experienced some form of rejection at some point in their lives and have not dealt with these feelings in a healthy way.

Violence against women, fired workers resorting to extremes of violence, and the case of the wife biting off the genitals of her adulterous husband[3], are just a few examples of the strong link between rejection and aggression in today's revenge prone and unforgiving society. However, much of that aggression elicited by rejection is also turned inward.

In extreme cases, many have resorted to suicide. Rejection sends us on a mission to seek and destroy our self-esteem. In a relationship rejection, it becomes easy to find fault in ourselves. We end up magnifying our own weaknesses or shortcomings, bemoaning all our inadequacies, kicking ourselves when we are already down, and beating our self-esteem to a pulp. The reason for rejection is a combination of a lot of factors such as a poor fit, wrong timing and the like. Blaming ourselves and attacking our self-worth only deepens the emotional pain we feel and makes it harder for us to recover emotionally. Sometimes even convincing ourselves, we are the only cause for the breakdown in our relationships, does not help. Even if others try to convince us otherwise, we may end up rejecting them. Certainly, when we are experiencing a painful rejection, thinking clearly is just not that easy.

Rejection does not respond to reason. Such is the effect of emotional rejection.

Spiritual effects of rejection

Is it right to spiritualise rejection? The simple answer is yes! Scripture warns us, we must not be ignorant of the devices of the enemy, *"… lest Satan should take advantage of us …"* (2 Corinthians 2:11) This means, we must be very much aware of who our number one enemy is, and be alert to what he is doing against us and be aware of his schemes and plans.

To every physical emotion there is a spiritual counterpart, and vice versa.

Look at it this way, evil spirits have their nature and will want to exhibit that nature in humans. So, a spirit of murder will want to cause people to be killed, to kill others or cause people to kill themselves. This is different from the spirit of death. This is because the spirit of death has different disguises, which are not limited to just the three things mentioned above. Anyway, without going into much depth on demonology, the spirit of rejection wants to ultimately victimise its victims by causing them to feel worthless and unwanted, thereby causing them to either reject God, reject others or reject themselves.

All that has been stated so far on rejection can be gleaned from the verse that *"the thief does not come except to steal, and to kill, and to destroy..."* (John 10:10). It is important to understand and take this warning seriously.

Always think of the enemy's end game. The plan is simple – divide and conquer, cause the children of God to be separated from their true Protector, cause them to be divided and lose faith, and cause them to destroy themselves as a result.

Every bad thing, every bad thought, every bad situation, indeed everything contrary to God's purpose is based on this simple plan. We have been given the counter-intelligence that:

> "... we do not wrestle against flesh and blood, but against principalities, against powers, against the rulers of the darkness of this age, against spiritual hosts of wickedness in the heavenly places."
>
> *(Ephesians 6:12)*

It's a war plan and so the enemy has deployed many agents, demons and evil human counterparts to bring this common goal to fruition. Hence the spirit of rejection is just playing its part in the war plan.

The spirit of rejection, with the assistance of self-pity, will seek to separate you for destruction in three ways: separation from God, from yourself and others.

Demons always operate in groups, so it will work with not only the spirit of self-pity but also with the spirits of pride, hatred, unforgiveness, despair, depression, hopelessness and suicide. This group is not exclusive because they are united in their cause to destroy God's creation. They are divided in nature but united in cause. For instance, a demon of pride will be proud in assuming he is better than other demons but willing to share his place with another demon if it means destroying the human victim together.

You can detect the workings of these spirits working in people and indeed yourself when you experience the feelings below:

- You are easily offended or embarrassed by discipline or correction.
- You think you can do a better job than the current leader or teacher if you are given the opportunity. Though this may not necessarily be a bad thing, when mixed with pride and looking down on others, it becomes perverted.
- You find yourself comparing your circumstances or situations with others, and you never seem to measure up.
- You feel rejected if you are not greeted or acknowledged by leadership, your peers or subordinates. Your pride is wounded.

- You are always trying to prove yourself in public. Self-image and self-preservation is very important to you over and above the truth or what is morally right.
- You are very self-conscious, and feel like you are on the outside looking in during interactions with people.
- You constantly seek the approval of others and suffer from people pleasing.
- You feel as if you missed out on life's opportunities and now it's too late and life is meaningless.
- No amount of encouragement is enough to convince you of your worth.
- You believe no one understands you, or what you are going through. Therefore, you cannot relate and refuse to relate with others.

Please understand, the above examples are not to demonise various situations in life. Going through any of the above or other similar circumstances does not mean one is possessed by demons. I am simply trying to draw your attention to a certain 'way of thinking', which is not helpful. These thoughts on their own are indeed just thoughts, but the moment it becomes domineering and controlling, then it is most likely, an evil spirit is present and influencing your thoughts.

Endnotes

1: Jennifer Warner, 'Pain Social Rejecon Have Similar Effect on Brain'. webmd.com/sex-relaonships/news/ 20110328/pain-social-rejecon-have-similar-effect-onbrain WebMD Health News Reviewed by Laura J. Marn, MD on August 02, 2010 (accessed March 27, 2019).

2: Youth Violence: A report of the Surgeon General' www.ncbi.nlm.nih.gov/books/NBK44293/ Office of the Surgeon General (US); 2001, (accessed April 17,2019).

3: www.worldnewsdailyreport.com/woman-arrested-foremasculang-cheang-husband-with-her-teeth/ (accessed March 27, 2019).

Chapter 3

How the spirit of
rejection operates

The best way to understand how an evil spirit comes into a persons' life is to look at some legal definitions.

Let us start by looking at trespassing. In legal terms, a trespasser is someone who, without permission or privileges granted by the owner, enters on to another's property intentionally. Consider the key words 'without permission' and 'intentionally'. They mean basically that you have not given permission for this person or people to come into your home or use your property, but they have intentionally come on or used it anyway. Of course, a person may wander onto your property by mistake, but if they remain on after being told of their trespass, then it is a crime. Make no mistake, no evil spirit 'unintentionally' trespasses. They are calculating and ruthless in their plans to intrude into your life and your destiny.

A trespasser may trespass in order to do something contrary to what the owner would approve of.

Likewise, upon trespassing into your life, a spirit of rejection only has the agenda to cause damage.

Once a person initially trespasses and there is no opposition or detection, they can potentially become squatters. That person becomes bolder and starts to feel 'at home' on another man's property. By common law, squatters can begin to acquire some rights of occupancy dependent on how long they have been on the property undetected or unopposed.[1]

Similarly, once an evil spirit gains occupancy and there is very little resistance, or it is not detected, it begins to feel at home and starts being legalistic and claiming the right of occupancy to be in the life of its victim.

> "… when He had come to the other side, to the country of the Gergesenes, there met Him two demon-possessed men, coming out of the tombs, exceedingly fierce, so no one could pass that way. And suddenly they cried out, saying, "What have we to do with You, Jesus, You Son of God. Have You come here to torment us before the time?"'
>
> *(Matthew 8:28-29)*

We see here, the demons knew their 'rights' in that they had a time appointed to them to be tormented. Demons are very legalistic in their approach.

A different scenario may unfold where you have invited a stranger to your home, because you feel they mean no harm or you only allow them to the front door for a short period of time, thinking you are under control. But soon after, the stranger starts to 'feel at home' and goes into your bedroom, eats your food, and even decides to move in permanently! To your horror, this stranger can no longer be controlled and even starts to invite other strangers into your home. Eventually you may be forced into isolation in your own home or you become broke and not recognise your house anymore. This is how a permitted but limited entry can become an intrusion but due to the initial permission, the stranger can claim the right to be there.

Likewise, you may initially 'try out' a new experience or sin that lets in an evil spirit. Because you reason, it's only a phase or a bad thought, you may entertain it. But you may end up losing control, and it invites other spirits in as mentioned above.

Similarly, there may be a situation where you invite in and 'form a bond' with a familiar person, whom you no longer regard as a stranger. Because you have become used to this person being around, you readily hand over the keys. By so doing, you have given this person the rights to your house, everything and everyone in it. Even if you change your mind, it will become difficult to get an eviction because legally you have given this person every right to be there:

> "When an unclean spirit goes out of a man, he goes through dry places, seeking rest, and finds none. Then he says, 'I will return to my house from which I came.' And when he comes, he finds it empty, swept, and put in order. Then he goes and takes with him seven other

spirits more wicked than himself, and they enter and
dwell there; and the last state of that man is worse than
the first. So shall it also be with this wicked generation."

(Matthew 12:43-45)

This is the kind of control every demon craves, complete
possession of the humans they encounter. These are extremely
difficult to get rid of as was illustrated by Jesus's encounter
with his disciples who tried and failed to cast out an unclean
spirit which had rendered its victim deaf and dumb:

"... and when He had come into the house, His disciples
asked Him privately, 'Why could we not cast it out?' so
He said to them, 'This kind can come out by nothing
but prayer and fasting.'"

(Mark 9:28-29)

There is yet another scenario where individuals leave the
door completely open to unwanted people or things,
knowingly or unknowingly. By so doing, they 'invite'
anyone and anything to come in.

This is what many refer to as being 'free-spirited' in
that there is no moral compass, nor barriers. They lead an
'anything goes', experimental life, with no self-control nor
constraints, allowing whatever spirit, good or bad, to move
freely in and out of their lives.

Finally, albeit not conclusively, another illustration of
how a spirit comes into one's life is when there is an opening,
a crack in the house. Again, it could be deliberate, but this is
mostly sometime due to carelessness or ignorance. A good
example is when mice come in through the skirting boards

or the cracks in the wall. They come in usually because the house is dirty, there are lots of dark corners or they have a connection in the house via a resident mother mouse.

To illustrate, could it be that your child is feeling suicidal because you left a crack in the wall of his/her spirit through exposure to negative words? Although suicide is a combination of a lot of factors, negative words can introduce negative spirits which cause rejection, and rejection can lead to suicide if not dealt with effectively. My life is an example of this. As I felt rejected due to negative words from my mother. I am sure it was not her intention to have such an effect on me, however words have a powerful effect on people especially if it is coming from someone in a position of trust.

As you will see from the non-exhaustive list below, many of us are unaware about the spiritual implications of the many experiences we have had in our lives that have become an opening for unwanted elements.

These spirits are bullies, and forceful. They are no respecter of persons and, like armed robbers, they will not desist from brutality to get what they want. Jesus warns, "... *the thief comes only to steal and kill and destroy; I have come that they may have life, and have it to the full.*" (John 10:10)

Experiences/doors that invite in the spirit of rejection

Generational/Parental influence

Rejection can be passed on from one generation to another just like an heirloom. Parents, often unknowingly through the words spoken over their children, have everlasting effects on their children including those not yet born. Parents are legal guardians of their God-given children. "*... for He shall give His angels charge over you, to keep you in all your ways.*" (Psalm 91:11) Everyone has guardian angels and even more so, a helpless foetus or young children who cannot pray or guard themselves from evil energy and forces. However, those who know right from wrong and are able to make decisions for themselves at whatever age, can give permission to these forces as explained above either by word, deed or implication. Upon granting this permission, you can effectively render your God-given guardian angel powerless or dormant in your life.

Just as a parent's permission is required to administer care for their children, a parent's permission is also required for these evil spirits to invade the life of a foetus or innocent child. So, through your words and actions as a parent, your child may be exposed to rejection.

Below are more examples of how rejection sets in:

* You were born as a result of an unwanted pregnancy – this is the most common but undetected way of entry. Scientifically, we learn that unborn children need happy hormones and they can sense when their mother is not happy. Projecting rejection, no matter how the child came to be, is an invitation by you as the parent for the spirit of rejection and so many others, to come into the child. You may also have been the child who was unwanted.

    I particularly experienced this myself. I was an unwanted pregnancy, which pre-disposed me to repeating the same cycle of mistakes. So, when

I became pregnant with my daughter, there was a 1 in 4 chance of a full Sickle Cell child since both my husband and I are both carriers of sickle cell traits. Though we were unsure how to take care of her financially and medically, I made sure to speak words of life and positivity over her.

- Your parents wanted a boy, but you were born a girl, and vice versa. Even your position in the family can expose you to rejection such as being a middle child, 'middle child syndrome' or a step-child.[2]
- You were adopted, and so feel rejected by your birth parents.
- One or both of your parents died when you were a child.
- Your parents got divorced.
- The absence of a parent, especially a father.
- Not feeling loved by either parent.
- Been abused by a parent or family members.

Relationship/ Marital influence

We are relational beings, and as aforementioned we want to belong to someone or somewhere or something. We devote ourselves, our time and resources to relationships in the hope our efforts will be reciprocated and appreciated. Insecurities, distrusts, unfaithfulness, and sexual immorality of all forms, could all be because of rejection in some way.

The spirit of rejection can come in through:

- Being dumped, refused or ridiculed by the opposite sex, especially in your teens. Everyone always remembers their first crush and first heartbreak. If this common experience is not dealt with effectively when it happens, it can shape your view of the opposite sex and your outlook on life forever when it comes to interacting with the opposite sex.

- Not being married and loneliness. Many are in perpetual state of depression and desperation because of this. It is as a response to this type of rejection that I believe many decide not to marry, cannot be faithful, and are distrusting and have commitment issues.

- A break up or divorce. A broken heart is like a broken hedge. Many things will creep in. Defences are down when one is heartbroken. Ironically those who have been divorced or heartbroken are more guarded than before yet open to the spirit of rejection, thereby making it difficult to love again.

Physical Influence

We are vain by fallen nature. No matter how redefined we are, our physical appearance, not necessarily what we put on, but how we are built matters to us. In our natural state, be it in our health or wealth, there are certain situations beyond our control that can cause the spirit of rejection take advantage of us, such as:

- Being born with a disability or deformity – I have often wondered why God would allow someone to be born with a deformity. I found the answer in Genesis – *"Then God saw everything that He had*

made, and indeed it was very good ..." (Genesis 1:31)
See everything God created is 'very good'. Anything
short of this description cannot be from Him.

However, there are circumstances where God may 'permit'
something that is not good to happen to His children. The
story of the man born blind (John 9:1-12) throws some
light on to these age-old questions: why was I born this
way? Why me? Why do bad things happen to good people?
A whole book could be written in an attempt to answer
these questions.

I would say, ultimately God knows best, He is God, we
have to trust His judgement and I believe no one can ever
really know why things happen the way they do. However,
God is not unjust or unfair. There is a reason and a purpose
to everything. Though we see in part, He will reveal all
things in due season and all things will work together for
our good in the end if we do not give up:

"Now as Jesus passed by, He saw a man who was blind
from birth and His disciples asked Him, saying, 'Rabbi,
who sinned, this man or his parents, that he was born
blind?' Jesus answered, "Neither this man nor his
parents sinned, but that the works of God should be
revealed in him.""

(John 9:1-3)

Jesus went on to heal this man which brought glory to
God.

One may ask why did God allow this man in the story
to be born blind in the first place, and why does God allow

birth defects? This is indeed a tough one to answer and I am sure many parents in this situation would have asked this question also. We can receive some guidance from the story of Adam and Eve in Genesis chapter 3 when they sinned against God through disobedience. We understand that as a result of their disobedience, sin entered the world and since then the human race has been plagued with evil, disease and death. *"When Adam sinned, sin entered the world. Adam's sin brought death, so death spread to everyone, for everyone sinned."* *(Romans 5:12).* So, one explanation is that birth defects happen because of sin, not necessarily due to the sins the parents committed or indeed that of the baby but because of 'Sin' itself. On the other hand, knowing the harassing and opportunist nature of the devil, it is possible that he cause a baby to deform in the mother's womb either because of sin, occultism or via an opening as previously described. The spirit of rejection will then capitalise on this disability or special birth situation and cause more damage.

The best way to explain this is from two perspectives:

1.   Sinful world

Though God is good and everything He creates is good, birth deformity is not God's plan of 'good'.

However, due to the effects of sin birth defects can occur. We live in a fallen, sinful world, at variance from God's original plan of perfection. Through the events in the Garden of Eden by Adam and Eve, sin entered the world and unfortunately that began the decline from humanity's perfection. All generations to follow have been under the curse of sin in this world. This means that when sin runs its course, deviations from God's perfect plan such as deformity can happen.

God wants us to be perfect as He is – *"But you are to be perfect, even as your Father in heaven is perfect." (Matthew 5:48)* Now this can mean many things, such as God wants us to be 'complete', 'whole', 'rounded', 'mature' as He is. However, it can also mean God wants us to aim for perfection. Yes, we have all fallen short of God's Glory *(Romans 3:23)* and no one is perfect but we are encouraged work at it: *"Don't copy the behaviour and customs of this world, but let God transform you into a new person by changing the way you think. Then you will learn to know God's will for you, which is good and pleasing and perfect." (Romans 12:2).* Therefore, it is possible to become *like* God in 'perfection' – *"… so all of us who have had that veil removed can see and reflect the glory of the Lord, and the Lord – who is the Spirit – makes us more and more like Him as we are changed into His glorious image." (2 Corinthians 3:18)*

God knows this is 'a hard nut to swallow' that's why He gives us grace and strength to keep at it if we don't give up. *"… for it is God who works in you both to will and to do for His good pleasure." (Philippians 2:13)*

His plan is first to give us the chance to choose Him willingly. He recognises we are cut off from Him and that we must choose what is right and what is wrong, sin or salvation, life or death, heaven or hell. By giving us the ability to choose, this means that He also allows the effects of our poor choices.

2.   Acts of Sin

If a mother takes illegal drugs during her pregnancy, there is a much higher risk she will give birth to a baby born with disabilities. A mother who smokes or drinks too much alcohol prior to or during the time of pregnancy, by so doing risks endangering the health of her unborn child. Even if parents are healthy when babies are conceived, they can still be the recipient of genetic defects that exist in family lines.

So, birth defects can be explained as the result of poor choices by others such as the prescription of the thalidomide drug to pregnant mothers or the poor health habits of fathers, which may then affect their babies' genes, as well as genetic alterations passed on to those who are otherwise innocent.

Below are some more examples of the physical factors which may lead to a spirit of rejection:

- Long-term illness: One can easily feel rejected by both God and man when you have a disease.
- Loss of someone close to you: this can be a child, husband, wife, mother, father, a good friend or even a pet. Again, the common question we ask in all this is 'Why me?' This question can be construed as selfish and arrogant in nature if we really pause to think properly about it. Why not you? What makes you and me so special to be exempt from the woes of this life? However, it is still a valid question, which God does answer. Though, it is often not the response we would like to hear.

- Your physical appearance: Not everyone will have the perfect head shape, hip line, slim build, the lists goes on. That is what makes us human, our differences and uniqueness. If we all looked the same, we would complain of lack of diversity. If we all had the perfect everything, we would reject God even more. The use of cosmetic surgery, make-up and other products are all ways to help our self-image and reduce rejection. Although mostly harmless, when heavily relied upon for self-confidence, they may create another unpleasant situation resulting from self-worship, pride, jealousy, vanity and the like.

- Your background/upbringing.

- Race/Skin colour.

- Educational background: This is in terms of your exposure in life. You may be excluded from certain jobs because you have no education or you have attained a certain level of education. The obvious 'fix' for this is to get educated; however, we must consider that whilst everyone has 'access' to education in modern society, some feel they do not 'fit' into the educational system. Indeed, not everyone can afford a higher level of education.

- Your spiritual upbringing or environment: the church environment without the Holy Spirit can cause a lot of rejection for people. Many come to the church lost and hopeless looking for a place to call home, only to be met by 'religious people' and hypocrites. The spirit of rejection takes advantage of this and makes people draw even farther away from God and His true church.

Fruits of rejection

Apart from other results of rejection, more fruits or effects of rejection are listed below:

- You search for love in the wrong places by engaging in all forms of sexual immorality, the use of drugs, alcohol, illegal substances, even self-harm.
- Negative and perverse desires. You constantly sabotage relationships with negativity.
- Condemnation. The disapproval of others affects you and enforces self-condemnation.
- Guilt. Constantly blaming yourself for being rejected or feeling rejected.
- Judging others to avoid being 'judged'.
- Worry and Hopelessness.
- Dissatisfaction and Perfectionism. Dissatisfied with what you have and always looking for perfection, which in itself can become an obsession. Leading to depression, discouragement, anxiety and fear of imperfection.
- Unforgiving of others, yourself and not willing to be open, confess sin.
- Constant fear of being disliked.
- Hatred of those who rejected you.
- Doubtful and distrusting of yourself, others and God.
- Accusations against God, yourself or others.
- Loneliness/isolation. Rejection by others can make you feel lonely or actively seek isolation from people or situations.

- Self-pity and low self-esteem. Rejection can hurt your ego and sense of pride.
- Jealousy and envy of those who were accepted.
- Uncertainty about your future and what will become of you. This means there is also fear of abandonment and fear of commitment.
- Control over others in order to make yourself feel better and mask your pain of rejection.

If you recognise these fruits in your life or loved ones, you may feel helpless and be wondering what to do. Until you are ready to break free and be delivered from the spiritual torment of rejection, it will continue to harass you with the intent of driving you to self-destruction.

Here are a few things you can do on your journey to freedom:

- Pray for God to give you the revelation of His unconditional love for "... but God demonstrates His own love toward us, in that while we were still sinners Christ died for us." *(Romans 5:8)*

Understand, there is nothing you can 'do' to earn His love. To draw an analogy, when I first held my daughter in my arms I did not give her a 'to do list' of what she needs to do in order to earn my love. The moment she was born, even whilst in the womb, I was already full of love for her. Likewise, allow that love from your heavenly Father to enter your heart today. Believe it, it's true!

John 3:16 states this clearly – God loves the world and everything in it, (including you and me). We do not need to meet a condition to earn His love but only to gain eternal life. To receive eternal life requires you believing in His Only Begotten Son, Jesus. Pray and decide to see others through the "Eyes of Christ"

> "… but the Lord said to Samuel, 'Do not look at his appearance or at his physical stature, because I have refused him. For the Lord does not see as man sees; for man looks at the outward appearance, but the Lord looks at the heart."
>
> *(1 Samuel 16:7)*

Our own expectations and standards can cause a lot of disappointment leading to an occasion to feel rejected. We must learn to see others for who they are, human, flawed but favoured nonetheless. We must look at others through the eyes of Christ; He looks at us and sees a message in our mess, a miracle in our mistakes, choosing to see a 'marred' person in need of mercy. Then Jesus said, *"Father, forgive them, for they do not know what they do."* (Luke 23:34)

Learn to objectively evaluate or process those who have rejected you, considering yourself. If you put yourself in the same position of that manager who had to let you go, would you have done the same; if roles were reversed would you have carried on with that marriage or relationship? What would Jesus do on this occasion? A truthful and Bible-based self-diagnosis will help streamline your feelings and expose elements of pride or hidden ulterior motives. This exercise should help to stop the adverse effects of rejection in its tracks. You may still feel rejected; however, the sting will be less and you will start to see the bright side of it.

Be conscious of negative words spoken either to you or by you over your life:

> "Death and life are in the power of the tongue, and those who love it will eat its fruit."
>
> *(Proverbs 18:21)*

It is important to pray against and reject the words, which don't build you up but tear you down. Every creature God created has a natural weapon of attack and defence. Generally, birds use their beaks to pick up food, but they also use it to attack their prey or as a defence against their predators. Lions use their mouths to pick up their cubs, but they also use the same mouth as a defence and attack against their hunters.

Likewise, as humans, who are on 'top of the food chain', our God-given weapon for defence is our tongue. One may argue, our brain is a weapon; after all we use our intellect to create weapons of defence and attack against our enemies. Whilst this view point holds true if your enemy is a fellow human, it is very limited in its scope because, how do you defend yourself against an enemy you cannot see physically? Or how do you use an AK 47 to shoot at an evil spirit that is harassing your soul? The human with all witty inventions is powerless against such enemies:

> "For we do not wrestle against flesh and blood, but against principalities, against powers, against the rulers of the darkness of this age, against spiritual host of wickedness in the heavenly places."
>
> *(Ephesians 6:12)*

However, thanks be to God that He gave us the power to tread upon spiritual scorpions and serpents and they shall no means hurt us:

> "Behold, I give you the authority to trample on serpents and scorpions, and over all the power of the enemy, and nothing shall by any means hurt you. Nevertheless, do not rejoice in this, that the spirits are subject to you, but rather rejoice because your names are written in heaven."
>
> *(Luke 10:19-20).*

Telling someone they are ugly and no good is hurtful and can lead to feelings of rejection and self-hatred. Perhaps you have opened yourself up for rejection and associated spirits because you constantly tell yourself you are ugly and a failure. You are by your own tongue attacking yourself. Speaking positive words means you are not only defending your heart against the attacks of negative words, you are also launching an assault on your enemies by confessing God's good Word and positivity over your life. Today, why not repent for any negative words or curses you have spoken over yourself or others in the past and break their hold over you. **Forgive those who have offended you**

> "… for if you forgive men their trespasses, your heavenly Father will also forgive you."
>
> *(Matthew 6:14)*

Remember not to forget to forgive those who have genuinely hurt you. This is regardless of whether they recognise and accept their wrong doing or not. When you read into the cause of the shootings in America, for example, you will notice that the motives of the shooters and their circumstances have common traits such as rejection, unforgiveness and revenge. They were either expelled, sacked or neglected. Now these are not the only causes of their behaviour; however, it is a contributory factor.

There may be someone who needs your forgiveness and you will also need the forgiveness of others. Look at situations in perspective! For example, if you are married, you have rejected all those you could potentially have married. You may have been rejected by one employer, but without the rejection you may not have found your calling.

Make a decision to overcome

> "He that overcomes shall inherit all things; and I will be
> his God, and he shall be my son."
>
> *(Revelation 21:7)*

You are very important to God so simply believe it. Understand that you are engaged in a battle for your soul; therefore, do not let past defeats cause you to quit. As you seek God first, He will direct your steps to further find the right counsel and deliverance. Rejection is a thief who wants to take your life from you slowly if given the chance.

It constantly seeks to expose its victims to rejection by influencing their decisions and clogging their minds. Rejection will also ensure you seek love in the wrong places and if you have experienced rejection before, like most of us have, you may soon also feel that God has rejected you and therefore pull away from God.

God is the only One who can save us from the devices of the enemy. We can overcome rejection! We only need to let go and let God. He will not save us from our friends or what we like. If you like the effects or the presence of rejection, you cannot be set free.

God, in His infinite mercy, has given us power over all evil, through His Son Jesus Christ. Therefore, we need only be equipped with this knowledge and then take the step of faith to apply what we know, so we may be free from the clutches of rejection.

How to fight and win the battle with rejection

Remember rejection is also a feeling of not being wanted or loved. It may also mean or it implies something or someone is 'not fit for use'. When this mind is in you, you generally tend to fight the people who genuinely mean well and those who love you for who you are. It is also likely, when you are eventually shown love, you will reject it. Ironically, you reject the thing you need the most. Therefore, it becomes necessary to tear down the wrong image of God, yourself and others, which the spirit of rejection has built in your thoughts and mind.

To do this, first you need to believe and accept God loves you unconditionally and you are accepted by Him! Ultimately, only His approval and validation should matter and it supersedes all others. Remember:

- God is love, He will not stop loving you!
- Love is patient, and God is not limited by time, so He has all the time in the universe to remind you just how much He loves you.

- God is far superior than all, so only what God says about you is true, not what you think and feel, and what others have said about you. So, let what God says about you be true, and all other words and thoughts, or what someone else has said negatively about you, be a lie! "... but let God be true, and every man a liar."

(Romans 3:4)

"There is no fear in love; but perfect love casts out fear, because fear involves torment. But he who fears has not been made perfect in love."

(1 John 4:18)

Think of it this way, if rejection were not a problem for you, how would you feel? Well, you would feel loved, accepted and happy. That is how God wants you to feel!

Call to Action

Speak to God audibly on how you feel about those who rejected you and about your experience. Express yourself and even feel free to cry to Him. Then allow Him to heal your heart. Why not say this prayer:

My Father in Heaven, please help me to let go of this hurt, help me to see the good in my experience. Teach me how to receive your love even as I overcome rejection, in Jesus' Name. Amen.

Endnotes

1: gov.uk/squang-law (accessed April 1, 2019).

2: Krisne Fellizar '7 Subtle Signs You're Suffering from Childhood Rejecon As an Adult' bustle.com/p/7subtle-signs-youre-suffering-from-childhood-rejeconas-adult-13197726, (accessed April 1, 2019).

Chapter 4

Betrayal

"When Jesus had said these things, He was troubled in spirit, and testified and said, 'Most assuredly, I say to you, one of you will betray Me.'"

(John 13:21)

Betrayal is an abuse of trust in general, abuse of the position of trust. It destroys the very foundation of trust. Betrayal is a form of death, something dies in you when betrayed; trust, self-worth, sometimes even hope dies. It carries with it the powerful mixture of emotions like loss or grief, confusion, self-blame, loneliness, anger, vulnerability, helplessness, exposure, self-righteousness, revenge, all leading ultimately to unforgiveness and bitterness, prejudice and in extreme cases, hatred and murder.

Each one of these emotions has its own level of intensity depending on the predisposition of the one betrayed, the surrounding circumstances and the support system available to that person. In this chapter I will express some of my own experiences of betrayal and its impact on my life. I will also share the practical ways in which God enabled me to overcome.

I am convinced most people, if not everyone, will at some point experience a form of betrayal, whether it is betrayal by the politicians you voted for or the deep disappointment felt at the departure of your favourite football player from your team. It is equally possible, you may end up being a betrayer as well as being betrayed.

My story

Dear reader, please note, I share my story not from the root of bitterness or disrespect to anyone but from a place of healing and freedom. I would not be able to share this if I were still bound by those dark feelings, which once plagued my soul. God has kept me and indeed enables me to also testify of His saving grace no matter the challenges in life. Also note, the characters in my story are also on their own journey and relationship with God. It is not my intention to taint their character though I admit, my personal account in the book will not explain their own point of view or portray their current state of mind. However, there is no way I will tell my story without mentioning some important people in my life and how their actions affected me.

I had a very challenging childhood, and did not have any role models to look up to as such. My mum, bless her, had me when she was 20 years old; she is a strong woman. She worked hard to see me through my education in the early years and I will forever be grateful to her for taking me to church, where I met God.

As a result of my childhood and the yearning I had to belong and to be loved, I formed a warped idea of what marriage would be like. I used the term 'warped' because it is only now that it became clear to me, I did not fully understand what marriage was before I got married. I had a tainted picture.

At a very young age I started building all these lofty ideas that my husband would be the answer to my prayers, he would indeed wipe away my tears and would fill the longing I had to be loved and cared for, he would remove the rejection I always felt growing up. I remember as a young girl, every time I had an issue with my family and felt mistreated, I would always imagine the day I would be with my future husband and how he would take care of me. I believed it.

Fast forward to age 22 at which point I was happily married to my soul mate. By the way I do not have second thoughts on marrying young, I believe it is good to marry young. Just make sure you are ready and mentally, physically, spiritually and financially mature, which means you are responsible and accountable for your actions. Being older does not equate to maturity. Anyway, we were happy, well, I thought we were. I never really had much suspicion of what was going on, and I was not one to snoop around or be controlling. I did not pay much attention to the 'signs'. There were years of feeling like something was 'off', always feeling alone even though I was married, emotionally blackmailed, it's like he was not my 'fan' – he did not readily talk excitedly about me. I felt as if I was a bother to expect certain qualities such as patience, tolerance and understanding as one would expect from a husband. Fine protocol will not permit me to elaborate on our marital sex life; however, suffice it to say that it wasn't what we both envisioned it to be. It later transpired, we both had deficiencies in our expectations and communication of our desires was implied and applied wrongly.

The mind, they say is a very powerful sex tool. If you get your mind where it needs to be – open and free sex will be enjoyable not abhorred.

I was in pain, it was not an enjoyable experience for me most of the time. I would cringe because my mind was now tainted with associating sex with pain due to the previous painful experiences, coupled with 'unexplainable' physical discomforts which turned out to be medical issues, which my husband later explained were from the 'other women'.

That was it. It all clicked, like a light switch coming on in a dark room of snakes! It suddenly made sense why I would feel insecure in my marriage or feel something was missing. Unbeknown to me, I was surrounded by traitors. The husband of my youth, the one I had so much trust in, was having an affair. He was having an affair with a lady in our local church, and someone I was close to. She was the only one present at the birth of our daughter. I welcomed her into my home as a younger sister, and she was supposedly a homeless orphan so I trusted her. I knew she had a sexually active life but didn't know, I was being fooled. It later transpired, they had been having affairs for over two years, in our house, on our marital bed and other adventurous places only the mind can imagine in our neighbourhood. At the time it all unfolded, I had been cheated on for a span of seven years of my eight-year marriage. He was having affairs not just with one person but with several other women – my work colleague, my fellow church members and those I do not know.

I felt my world crumbling down all around me as if I had just been hit by a tornado or had a tooth yanked out of my mouth with no anaesthetic. Yes, the pain I felt was blinding.

So how did I find out?

Well, I had my intuition but dismissed it. However, when God says It's enough, it's enough. God directed me to the truth Himself. Others knew what was going on but felt it was best to withhold the information from me. I'm not sure I would have done the same, but God knows best. One Sunday morning as I was getting ready for church, my husband was asleep. He very rarely leaves his phone lying around but, on that day, he left it in the dining area downstairs. The phone alarm went off, so I went to turn it off. Then I heard a voice asking me to open the messages that had popped up. I did. What happened next shook me to the core.

I have since been able to and still am, processing the very many emotions and thought processes that I went through. It's an experience which is one of the most devastating forms of pain that can be inflicted upon a person. The more trusted, the betrayer, the more painful and unbearable the betrayal is to the one betrayed.

The more oblivious or unrepentant the betrayer is, the more pain is inflicted on the betrayed. The word inflict suggests, it's in most cases, a deliberate act by one person, or if not deliberate – a reckless act.

For example, being betrayed by a manager who promised promotion to you but then side-lined you for someone else is not likely to lead to hatred and murder. It may however lead to loss of trust, low self-confidence and confusion. On the other hand, someone who is molested by a parent or a person in a position of trust may well be enraged by this betrayal which can then lead to several reactions, one of which is murder.

The Bible enlightens us on this subject and, like other lessons to be learnt, we are given real examples of people who experienced betrayal in one shape or another and to varying degrees.

Jesus – betrayed by His disciple, companion, worker and 'brother' Judas.

Jesus knows the pain of betrayal first hand. He was ultimately betrayed by those he came to live and die for. Humanity betrayed Him. I betrayed Him. However, I suppose the most documented betrayal of all, deemed to be the worst and most treacherous betrayal of all time, was Judas's betrayal of Jesus for thirty pieces of silver.

> "Then one of the twelve, called Judas Iscariot, went to the chief priests and said, 'What are you willing to give me if I deliver Him to you?' and they counted out to him thirty pieces of silver. So, from that time he sought opportunity to betray Him."
>
> *(Matthew 26:15)*

"… then Judas, His betrayer, seeing that He had been
condemned, was remorseful and brought back the
thirty pieces of silver to the chief priests and elders,
saying, ' have sinned by betraying innocent blood.' and
they said, 'What is that to us? You see to it!'"

(Matthew 27:3)

"… even my own familiar friend in whom I trusted,
who ate my bread, has lifted up his heel against me."
(Psalm 41:9 see John 13:18)

But Jesus did not become vindictive, bitter, or angry.
Quite the opposite. After receiving the traitor's kiss, Jesus
addressed Judas as "friend".

"… and while He was still speaking, behold, Judas, one of
the twelve, with a great multitude with swords and clubs,
came from the chief priests and elders of the people. Now
His betrayer had given them a sign, saying, 'Whomever
I kiss, He is the One; seize Him.' Immediately he went
up to Jesus and said, 'Greetings, Rabbi!' and kissed Him.
But Jesus said to him, 'Friend, why have you come?'
Then they came and laid hands-on Jesus and took Him."
(Matthew 26:47-50)

Before we can truly appreciate Jesus's sacrifice for us, we
must first understand, we are all lovers of ourselves like
Judas. Indeed, we have been shown mercy and that's why
we can also be called friends of Christ.

This is precisely why Jesus is no ordinary Man. He
displayed the greatest level of selflessness even in the face of

the agonising pain of betrayal and rejection suffered at the hands of those He called His own.

There is much to write about how Jesus handled his traitors but one thing is certain, Jesus focused on His purpose. If he had allowed His emotions and righteous anger to seek revenge or justification/vindication, perhaps His purpose may not have been accomplished in the destined manner. Betrayal has the far-reaching effect of changing one's destiny if not properly handled.

Jesus wisely looked beyond the immediate pain to the lasting praise of His Father in accomplishing His mission on earth for mankind to be reconciled with God.

Jesus looked beyond and saw the victory and declared *"It is finished!"* meaning – it is done, accomplished! He looked at those who betrayed Him in the past, present and future –all of us wretched sinners and declared – the Debt is payed! The Father is obeyed and glorified! God be praised!

> "So, when Jesus had received the sour wine, He said, 'It is finished!' and bowing His head, He gave up His spirit."
>
> *(John 19:30)*

David was no stranger to betrayal

> "If an enemy were insulting me, I could endure it; if a foe were raising himself against me, I could hide from him. But it is you, a man like myself, my companion, my close friend, with whom I once enjoyed sweet fellowship as we walked with the throng at the house of God."
>
> *(Psalm 55:12-14)*

Most likely the close friend was Ahithophel, David's close counsellor who also counselled Absalom's to betray his father. (see 2 Samuel 15-17)

Ahithophel's counsel was as sure as an oracle. He was implicitly trusted by David; in fact, David overcame many situations with Ahithophel by his side. Ahithophel may have had some unchecked hurt against David for some of his actions, so he decided to join David's rebellious son, Absalom, in a campaign to take over the throne. Ahithophel was so consumed with destroying David that he counselled Absalom on how to target David when his guard was down.

But David, heartbroken that his friend and counsel has joined forces with his own son to betray him, prayed that the counsel/advice of Ahithophel would be rejected. And so, it was that for the first time ever in his life, Ahithophel's advice was not taken; David knew Absalom would have succeeded had he listened and now he would fail. With his pride wounded and ashamed, Ahithophel took his own life. The closer the relationship, the greater the pain of betrayal.

In Psalm 55 David laments a broken trust, he hints at how to overcome the pain. In victory He writes:

> "But I call to God, and the LORD saves me. Evening, morning and noon I cry out in distress, and He hears my voice."
>
> *(Psalm 55:16-17)*

Samson – betrayed by his lover, Delilah

Samson fell for Delilah – oh how she captivated him! Like most of us, he also experienced a painful betrayal in his relationship, which would cost him his dignity, anointing, physical sight and eventually, his life. Let's look into the story of Samson and Delilah a little bit more as it will give us a better understanding of the effects of betrayal in a relationship.

Delilah was approached by the rulers of the Philistines with a bribe – if she told them the secret of Samson's strength, they would pay her 1,100 pieces of silver. On three occasions, she pleaded with Samson to divulge his secret to her, and on three occasions he told her riddles which were far from the truth because she tested them out. She nagged him day and night, to the point of accusing him of not truly loving her because he withheld this secret from her. Finally, he gave in and confided to her that the secret of his strength was in his hair, which had never been cut with a razor. She revealed the secret to the Philistine rulers who were able to capture and imprison Samson, and they gouged out his eyes believing that he would never be able to fight against them again. In this cunning way, Samson was betrayed by his lover and the love of his life. When Samson's hair grew back, he prayed to God to restore his strength so he could wreak revenge on his enemies. Although he was not able to secure his freedom, he seized the opportunity to push down the walls of the temple during one of their pagan festivities thereby killing over three thousand philistines who had gathered for the celebration. As a warrior and defender of Israel, he achieved more in his death than in life. *(Judges 16:4-28).*

Many would say, perhaps Samson had it coming, why would you trust someone not from your hometown, not a Christian like you, a known deceiver, and a prostitute who has tried on several occasions to let your enemies catch you? Why wasn't Samson bold and wise to get rid of her when he could? Why did God not stop him from meeting such a conniving woman?

Perhaps when we get to heaven, we will be able to ask him!

Having been in a very similar position myself, I have come to understand Samson in a different way. The truth is, you will never know how you will react to betrayal of this kind until you experience it first hand, only God can and will give us the grace to overcome and heal.

Notice how Samson was able to rise above the betrayal of his lover by going to God for strength. Indeed, God granted his prayers, though it cost him his life at a relatively young age he was still able to accomplish something great for God – The destruction of the pagan temple and Israel's enemies.

Betrayal can be akin to death. I grieved the death of trust, I mourned the concept of true love and I buried the possibility of finding true happiness in marriage.

Expert, Jennie Wright-Parker, explains, there are seven stages of grief. I will attempt to explain my experience of betrayal using each stage of the grieving process.[1]

Shock and Denial

I was in shock alright! Learning of my husband's infidelity and unfaithfulness was indeed enough to shock me to the very atom of my being. I could not believe it was happening to me. I have watched movies of it happening, I have heard of real-life people with infidelity issues, I have heard some of my own family members being accused of promiscuity, but never did I contemplate that I would one day be a victim of such brutal betrayal. I was just shocked. The lies, the pretence, the perpetual lies. It was all so unbelievable.

I actually went to church that fateful day. I mounted the pulpit and preached to God's people as I have always done, as if nothing was happening. From the outside it was not obvious what I was going through on the inside. How many of us like to wear our hearts on our faces, to let everyone know we are having a bad day. It takes maturity to be able to go through things and not burden others with it, thereby preventing people from feeling uncomfortable around you.

Friends, if you receive shocking news, you must find a way to let it out without letting people bear the brunt of your agony. It does not mean you suffer in silence or pretend as though everything is alright.

Share with wisdom and care. Being under pressure does not mean putting others under pressure on purpose. If they truly care for you, they will feel your pain without you forcing it on them.

Though I carried on with my life as normal I was still in shock, and even now I still get the aftershock sometimes, especially when I see some of these other ladies or see the places they have 'been' at.

I was in denial. I denied myself the chance to fully comprehend what had happened and how it would change my life forever. I pretended I was listening to others talk about their issues, and I did not fully accept, I was the one going through this mess and kidded myself it was someone else and I had to be strong for them.

Pain and Guilt

As the shock wore off, it was replaced by the feeling of incredible pain and suffering. My heart ached so much I thought I would collapse. It is a pain like no other. Indeed, it felt like someone close to me had died. I felt numb inside.

Imagine how Jesus felt when on His journey to the Cross. He would have met many people He prayed for, healed and saved and these same people are were the ones calling for him to die.

Imagine how Jesus felt when the person He chose to be his disciple was the very person who betrayed Him. All of a sudden my childhood torments of insecurities and rejection returned in full force. I had felt alone and unwanted before but this was ninety times worse. The pain was excruciating and unbearable. To a few, my pain was perhaps evident but to many people it was unknown. I still went to church, still ministered to God's people, still organised church events, and visitation, carrying on with everything to this day. I did not let it break my stride, but if you had looked closely you would have seen a wounded soldier.

You see I understood to an extent what the devil wanted me to do – quit. That's just it, I was left with almost no choice but to quit everything – church, motherhood, marriage, life. Though I could have taken a break from ministry to mourn my losses and 'fix' myself or my marriage, I knew if I did that, there was a high chance depression and defeat would get the best of me and I might never get up again. So, I did the opposite of what I felt like doing at the time. I carried on, and to the outside world, nothing had happened. My husband and I even went on to record together – our first EP.

It is very important we understand that true character is depicted by just how much you can understand and control your emotions, and the ability to separate your emotions from reality.

I felt a mixture of guilt and shame. Guilt because I felt or was made to feel that if a man cheats on his wife, it is because she drove him to that point by being beastly and cantankerous.

I reasoned, either I was disastrous in bed and not satisfying, or I was not sufficiently beautiful, fun, adventurous or sensual. So, I started to hear these voices blaming me for his actions. I knew he was sexually active from his past and, though from my past I was not a sexual novice either, I felt perhaps I had failed him sexually.

Pain and guilt for all the right and wrong reasons muddled up together is a recipe for suicidal thoughts.

Anger and Bargaining

All of a sudden it dawned on me just what had happened to me. I became very angry, with God, myself, my husband and those with whom he had had affairs.

I was angry with God because I kept thinking 'surely I prayed before marrying him. I had even asked my pastors to pray on my engagement ring!' So, why did God allow this to happen to me? What wrong did I do for showing kindness to a homeless Christian sister whose parents had both died, allowing her into my life and my home only to be betrayed in the most disgusting manner?

I was angry with myself because, I had turned a blind eye to an obvious weakness of character in my husband

and in myself for that matter. I should have known. I could have been more careful. I was too quick to overlook serious causes for concerns at the onset of our relationship, trusting and forgiving too easily. Why did I ever get married? Why me? Why him? Why now? So many questions but no answer was satisfying.

I was angry with my husband for obvious reasons, but mostly because I felt disgraced and degraded, insulted by his actions to say the least. I was angry with him also because of what we had lost. I knew nothing would ever be the same, and the blissfulness of marriage at the beginning was gone forever because of this unfortunate turn of events.

I was angry with the other women because, most of them were known to me, and they were 'sisters in Christ'. How could people be so evil and heartless? I went out of my way to befriend them and just be a Christian to them. What did I ever do to deserve such treatment?

So many questions plagued my mind, and the more I tried to understand, the angrier I became. So, I decided to bargain with God to just let me get past these dark days, months and years so that I could one day be genuinely happy and trusting again. Yet still I resolved to trust in Him.

Depression, Reflection, Loneliness

After a year or two, just when I thought I was getting on with my life, still married, trying to work things out, (at least so I thought), I found out my husband carried on having affairs and many other revelations came to light.

Funnily enough, I did not react as I did the first time. I was just numb and I believe God and the Holy Spirit gave me a really strong guardian angel to help me because I do not know how else I was able to keep a straight head. I don't think I revealed this new development to anyone till after six months had passed. In fact, the only reason I started telling people was because he started having affairs again and I just wanted someone else to bear the burden of helping him.

I went through some momentary bouts of depression. I remember one day after crying and feeling lost, I heard a voice urging me to kill myself and end the shame, then just at the same time, I saw my death play out, its effect on my daughter and God's judgement of hell for committing suicide.

After playing out the whole scenario and its effects I literally and audibly laughed out loud. When I came to myself, I told the voice to stop lying because no one was worth me dying for except Jesus. I chuckled at the game the evil voice was playing with me, and was sure it felt embarrassed for suggesting such a thing. God's love and judgement were all I could muster up to stop me from seriously considering suicide. Even as I write, I hear that same voice of despair.

A long period of sad reflection overwhelmed me when my guard was down. I have been blessed to have a lot of well-wishers and people who encouraged me, but it came to a point where I had to just look to God to pull me through. I allowed myself to grieve and mourn for lost love and wasted years. Now when people ask if am ok and I tell them I'll be alright, I mean it.

The Upward Turn

I started to adjust to people knowing of my marital crisis and started looking for the bright side of life. I started to become at peace with myself, knowing there is nothing I can do to fix my husband's seemingly insatiable desires or indeed my own feelings of loneliness than to pray and keep doing what I do for God. I was no longer afraid to show weakness or allow myself to be consoled. I had to live with my husband with the knowledge we were just cohabiting but not as a happy family. I had to be contented with this and for a moment we found peace and some light returned to our home.

Reconstruction and Reunification

Our broken marriage was gradually becoming more functional, and God was working on our minds. We started to find ways in which we could both get over the depths of separation we had experienced and start to re-build again, albeit slowly.

Acceptance and Hope

Going through all this at the same time stretched me spiritually. Sadness had birthed in me a new resolve to be closer to God. I felt strengthened, I started to learn to accept and deal with the reality of my situation. I was not happy but I had the joy of God's grace. Acceptance did not necessarily mean instant happiness for me, just the assurance of God's grace to see me through. Given the pain and turmoil I experienced, I know I can never fully understand the workings of God's Mighty hand. I will never be the same naive, carefree person I must have been in years long ago. But God will help me find a way forward.

As I journeyed through the roller-coaster of emotions and experiences, I can honestly say I have discovered more of God in my pain than in my praise. I remember being asked once before what I would do if someone cheated on me. I gave the answer most people would give, filled with indignation and all sorts of threats for the perpetrator. However, the truth is, you may never know how you would react till it happens to you.

Nothing prepares you for such a level of pain, just like no matter how 'ready' and 'mature' you feel to handle childbirth, even after you have been through it before, the pain is still indescribable. You never truly know how you will handle a situation until you are in it, acting out the movie of your life with no cue or props. I experienced all this before the age of 30, and so I feel older beyond my years.

Beloved, there is so much I learnt from my experience that I pray God helps me to share. I pray you will also be blessed and encouraged to face life's challenges without losing your faith in God or counting yourself out of the race of life.

There are indeed many self-help and motivational books out there, which might have more practical steps on what to do in this situation. However, God laid on my heart to share a few points on some of the things I did or thought of in my experience. There are of course many more; however, if you are like myself and you find yourself in a similar situation, then perhaps the steps below can help you deal with what you are going through:

- **Always remember that God loves you and wants you** – this may seem like some cliché statement that charismatic Christians throw around to disarm their listeners; but it is actually fundamental to understand and believe God indeed loves you and wants you. There is high price paid for you and God is not ready to let you go. Even if you are the offender, He still loves you, you only need to find your way back to Him in time. One of the most poignant feelings I had and, if I am honest, it still sometimes creeps up on me, is that feeling of being unloved and unwanted. I mean if the husband of my youth could find it easy to have affairs with several women whom he claims were not necessarily as beautiful or smart as I am, then I do not know who else could love me just as I am. My own mother informed me long ago that I was born as a result of a failed abortion attempt. Many have since disqualified me or dismissed me along the way. One major discovery and anchor for my soul was that indeed, Jesus loves me. Not only does the Bible tell me so, but I can see it could have been worse. Which brings me swiftly to the next point.

- **Learn to put things in context** – in the grand scheme of things that could possibly go wrong, what we go through at times is little in comparison. You see I used to be one of those who thought an unfaithful spouse is the worst thing that could happen, and if it happens it would be like an apocalypse. No, there are much worse things that could happen, the main one is death without accepting Christ. Can you imagine suffering on this earth and then dying only to realise there is a God and He sentences you to eternal condemnation because of unbelief and disobedience. That is a double jeopardy, and you will never forgive yourself for eternity. In fact, all the suffering of this world will fade in comparison! This is what helps me get over myself. There are also many people who are dealing with a painful health diagnosis or condition such that my situation will dim in their eyes compared to theirs. You just can never tell. Therefore, do not attempt to write off your situation as if it's the end of the world, it really and truly could be worse. God will not allow you to go through what He knows you cannot handle, doing so would make Him a mean God. He is a just and compassionate God who sees the end of a situation even before it starts.

- **Try your best to look inward** – honest self-diagnosis is liberating. It is better to know your strengths and weakness and accept there is room for change; and in areas beyond your control, accepting that only God can help. When my husband initially laid the blame for his actions on my doorsteps, I accepted it at first, and it wounded my self-confidence, and pride as a woman. I started to look inward but to the wrong things and I was looking inwardly through the eyes of others not through God's eyes. I saw my short comings as uglier than ever, and I felt something must be wrong with me to deserve such a treatment. It was later that the sweet Holy-Spirit began to comfort me and teach me that though I could have done better, same as anyone who is married, I needed to recognise where my faults end and where my husband's start. Also, I needed to recognise, I did better than most would in my circumstance. Therefore, I freed myself from self-blame and self-shame because I recognised the God in me.

If you are the culprit, it is important to accept your wrong and move on. Looking inward and upwards will help you move towards humility and freedom. A doctor will always ask to look 'into' the body in order to rightly diagnose and prescribe a cure for an ailment. Owning your actions and owning your need for God's help and saving grace is key to recovery and self-forgiveness.

It is important to look inward for two things: The God in you and the human in you. Even though Jesus was far more superior than we are, we must believe He understood that the human body was prone to sin. Therefore, He had to control the human desires/flesh in order to overcome temptation. The devil also knew this; hence he sought every opportunity to tempt Jesus with the same temptation of Adam: Lust of the eyes, Lust of Flesh and Pride of Life. Thanks be to God that Jesus succeeded in resisting the devil where Adam failed.

All through His ministry Jesus recognised the weakness of human nature as well as recognised the 'superior nature' of God in Himself. In order for us to overcome and learn from our experiences, we must also do the same. We must identify and accept our strengths and weakness. I had to understand this the hard way but thank God I did, and I pray you will also.

- **Consider yourself in your judgement of others** – this is similar to some of the points above. But I speak specifically of the power to forgive and if it is possible or practical to do so, endeavour to restore others in love. When you exercise physically, especially if it is for the first time or you do it irregularly, you'll discover some muscles you never imagined were there before! These can be most painful yet bittersweet at the same time. This is how I felt and still feel at times whilst going through this ordeal. I never knew how much I could forgive or just how wide my heart could expand to accommodate the very things I thought I could never tolerate. I was shocked to learn the depth of my capacity to love the unlovable or the length of my patient endurance.

Guess what? I still do not know in full just how much pain I can bear as a human being without losing my mind, but I think I have a fair idea.

A woman's uterus expands and her body changes to accommodate the baby she carries as it grows through several stages and trimesters. Similarly, I felt the 'stretch marks', the pull and tugs at my heart, mind and soul as if God was literally stretching me to my limits in order to grow and 'carry' what would be a great testimony of how He brought me through it all.

At one point I had to be a friend to my husband and not a wife as such. That was the only way I could not become an emotional wreck in the times he would leave us to go somewhere, or after he had made a confession of something else, he had just done. I had to see him as a lost soul who is precious to God in dire need of finding his way back home. I had to learn how to deal with the demon and not the man. Battling the temptations of self-righteousness as opposed to brotherly kindness, I learnt how to detach my emotions from the task at hand so all else would not crumble.

Oh, the most painful excruciating part is preaching through the pain. I did not stop preaching but I took time off work as I could not concentrate. It continued for a long time and it affected my job to an extent. I kept failing my professional exams. It was indeed another low point in my life but I did not stop doing outreach, and other church activities. Most of my church members didn't know, week in week out I preached to them as a wounded but protected soldier. I just could not give up. I needed the people as much as they needed me.

There are times I would be in church or counselling people and I would not know where my husband was or I would have just received a shocking discovery about my husband.

I had to carefully consider myself in order to find some grounds to forgive and let go of the bitterness that would build up in my heart. I considered the finished work of Jesus Christ on the Cross just for me. Where would I be if Jesus did not give me a chance to change? How can I ever repay Him for laying down His life for a wretched, murderous and unworthy sinner like me.

What I have done to Jesus is far more and worse than what anyone could ever do to me. And if Jesus could still forgive His persecutors, His betrayers, and His murderers whilst on the Cross then there is no one unqualified for my forgiveness. Alas that 'stretch mark' has changed my life forever. I get to see the world a bit more through the eyes of Jesus and the Father, wishing and hoping the 'prodigal child' in my husband will come home.

That is the reason why, though my husband had told me of a colourful past that would make any one cringe, I did not cringe. I rather chose to see the good and the 'could be'. Considering myself in light of what Jesus did for me was the reason I could stay in my marriage at the time even though I almost lost hope he could change. Years later, something else happened. I went from hope to despair again and it carried on like this for more than two years. Then, it happened, I had to come to terms with the consequence of my choice of husband.

See, the Holy Spirit showed me the difference between loving a person and having pity for them. I care for my husband, I love him as a brother, as a friend, we get along just fine even in ministry, but perhaps it is just what it was, and should have left it at that. I realised I could not bring myself to really vent the full brunt of my anger at him, not because

I couldn't but because I was always conscious of the effect that would have on his faith and his belief in God and his perception of what Christianity is. I was nurturing his faith; hence he could not fully commit to me or to a Christian 'marriage' because he is yet to discover just what that is. So, it becomes hard to blame someone who does not know what he should be doing. He cannot fully love me till he loves God.

I cannot be his spiritual mentor and his wife; I realised my love for him also meant I would have to let him go with no ill feelings. We were both victims of circumstances, but I am choosing to be victorious in forgiveness.

There is one thing I know for sure, whether you are the one betrayed or you are the betrayer, there is hope for redemption and restoration only if we put our trust in God.

Betrayal is a very strong emotion and it takes an even stronger emotion to overcome it. You may be feeling the hurt of being betrayed and the disappointment or shame of being the betrayer, but the stronger emotion that can conquer betrayal is love. Love conquers all.

I pray, as you read this book, you will receive healing and the grace to overcome the hurt and the wounds of a broken heart; that the love of God will flood your heart wherever you are and whatever you have been through. May the love of God touch your heart right now and set you free from pain and betrayal, in Jesus' name, Amen.

Call to Action

Be honest with yourself.

- Write down the names of the people you feel have betrayed you.
- Imagine that person is sat in front of you, what would you tell them now?
- Imagine you are the one who has betrayed someone. How would you like to be treated?
- Finally, imagine Jesus is in front of you. What would you say to him about how you feel?
- Remember to really let it out, and rest assured – God is listening.

Endnotes

1: recover-from-grief.com/7-stages-of-grief.html-Jennie Wright-Parker RN, MSCC, GC-C, (accessed April 2, 2019).

Chapter 5

Identity Crisis – Who Are You?

A person's identity cannot be easily defined by just one thing. There are many attributes, which make up a person such as feelings, ideas, perceptions, imaginations, desires, experiences, culture, education, background and so on.

At any point in life an 'identity crisis' may arise. This is the point where there is a battle between destiny and circumstance; where you know there is more to you, but your circumstances tell you differently.

My mum had me at 20 years old. I am sure it must have been hard for her being a young mum in those days. She still wanted to live her life as she saw fit, meaning I had to be 'out of the picture' in some way. I remember living with different family members, going to different schools and never really connecting with anyone.

Growing up I had to figure things out on my own. I did not have a relationship with my father, but I had many 'dads'; my mum was also trying to find herself so as a result I was subjected to many scenarios of what an ideal family could be. I was very smart as a kid in terms of standing up for myself and knowing when an adult was trying to deceive me. I was indeed very sharp-tongued and most of all I had a very good memory. I could retain memories of the minutest things a child should not be able to remember. It is to the Glory of God that I overcame most of the unpleasant memories of my childhood.

Rejection is a spirit. If you ever get pregnant out of wedlock or you have a baby with medical challenges, please try to get some good counselling and help, because you invite in to the child a spirit of rejection every time you express your desire not to have a child at a young age, out of wedlock or a child with special needs. As I said before, parents are also responsible for the spiritual well-being of their children. Evil spirits are legalistic. They will look for a legal right to be where they are, so although a child does not know what is happening and vulnerable, they will use the confession of the parents as a legal warrant to be in the child.

The Word of God is powerful and sharp and effective to break the hold of demonic influence. If you find yourself in an unwanted situation, please do not make it worse by speaking negatively. Confess positive words over your life and that of those who concern you: "Death and life are in the power of the tongue: and they that love it shall eat the fruit thereof."

(Proverbs 18:21)

I dealt with the spirit of legalistic rejection throughout my entire childhood. If I am very honest, at times it rears its head even in my adult life. Back then my relationship with God was not as deep; I just knew at the back of my mind there was more to life. I was lonely and felt like an ugly duckling and someone no one wanted to associate with. I even felt my mother saw me as a liability more than a responsibility.

The thoughts of suicide were a constant companion but deep in my heart I knew there was more benefit in staying alive than giving in. Parents, please never underestimate the power of complimenting your children. I never really had any compliments or 'reward' for good behaviour. I was only used to the negative comments about my appearance and my shortcomings. This built up in me a lot of bitterness towards my mum and immediate family.

At the age of 9, I was exposed to sexual exploitation and molestation. I was looking for something, did not know what or how to get it. I just gave in to whatever came my way. I lived in Amsterdam for a short while and by the age of 13, I was exposed to porn and other sexual practices. Though I was not 'fully into it', I thought I was in control. It is now when I look back that I can see God's hand over me, not letting go of me and not letting it have control over me. I have a very strong personality. If I am sold out on something, it will take a lot to convince me otherwise. So, I believe God did not let me really get sold out to the world or addicted to any of these things or else I would be a satanic agent by now.

I didn't know my identity at school; I just felt I needed to fit in somehow. I would hang out with girls who smoked at lunch time, even though I never smoked. I just did not want to be on my own looking like a 'loner'. I would sometimes even spend some of my break time in a toilet cubicle. I knew there was more to my life but my circumstances told me I was nothing. I would cry desperately looking for a way to be rid of the life I lived.

One thing my mum did, which helped me was to take me to church. This is where I found solace. I found my identity in Christ.

I started becoming conscious of the power and presence of God. I started understanding, being alone is not that bad. I started embracing my differences as what they were – just differences. We all cannot be the same, what a boring world that would be! God has a great sense of humour. He makes everyone the same yet we are all different, no one is completely satisfied or content except it is in Him. What makes you special is a combination of all the factors which make you different – your short comings, experiences and views on life.

I realised, I can only truly be myself when I know who I am in Christ. Anyone who knows me would agree, I am not afraid to talk to anyone. I always have something to say, I will find something to relate with. I did not get to this point of boldness in one day; I am still discovering what God is doing to me and through me.

I have seen many people who are stuck in an identity crisis not knowing who they are and what they are made of. We live in a society that encourages external validation. If you don't get many likes for your photo on a social media page, you might conclude that perhaps you are not beautiful or cool enough. The need for social approval has become a driving force for us, even for Christians. Compromise is now a norm, complacency is the order of the day. Though many are in God's house, they may still be lost.

You do not have to have life all figured out before you can find your identity. Going through the various trials and challenges are all part of the process. Your identity is in Christ Jesus, and knowing that you are a child of God. This is a fact that will never change unless you deny God. Everything that happens to us in this life is only supposed to make us draw strength from this blessed assurance, that Jesus is yours and you are for Jesus. Even after coming to Christ, it is important to know what God wants you to do.

Specifically, because this can lead to doing the wrong things for the right reasons, but wasting time all the same. We are encouraged by the apostle James with the following:

> "Dear brothers and sisters, when troubles of any kind come your way, consider it an opportunity for great joy. For you know that when your faith is tested, your endurance has a chance to grow. So let it grow, for when your endurance is fully developed, you will be perfect and complete, needing nothing."
>
> *(James 1:2 NLT)*

- You will have many temptations, accept it, expect it and process what you experience properly. The presence of God in your life does not mean the absence of temptation. The Bible is written for our example:

"All scripture is given by inspiration of God, and is profitable for doctrine, for reproof, for correction for instruction in righteousness, that the man of God may be perfect, thoroughly furnished unto all good works."

(2 Timothy 3:16)

- It is not the number of temptations or the severity of your trials, which makes you great it is the ability to endure till the end. God will surely see you through them all. We can confidently affirm that *"many are the afflictions of the righteous: but the Lord delivered him out of them all."* (Psalm 34:19)

    It is important for you to understand that your present situation is not your destination. God said in Hosea *"My people are destroyed for lack of knowledge …"* (Hosea 4:6) The devil will do anything to keep the knowledge of God's promises from you. That's why when we go through tough times, we are tempted to shut out God's Word and try to fix things ourselves. Allow yourself to be reminded, what you are going through is not the final chapter, it is not the end. It is only part of a story of victory, which is constantly being written. You might feel nothing is happening but God is working out patience in you through your problems. How will you know how strong your faith is if it has never been tested? How will you know you are going to another level if your faith is not being tested over and over again?

- There is no such thing as a wasted experience. Every experience can be used as a stepping stone to growth. It can however become a recurring experience if you did not learn anything the first time. The devil can also use your trials as a means of instilling fear in you so you never try anything new, never trust again, and never live life to its fullness. This is why it is very important to really know and fully comprehend that *"... the thoughts I [God] have for you ... thoughts of peace, and not of evil, to give you an expected end."* (Jeremiah 29:11) The presence of problems is not the absence of God, problems are just a faith-strengthening mechanism. God is not evil; He does not take a sickening pleasure in our demise just to prove a point. No, that is not God Almighty. His Word re-assures us:

"... there hath no temptation taken you but such as is common to man: but God is faithful, who will not suffer you to be tempted above that ye are able; but will with the temptation also make a way to escape, that ye may be able to bear it."

(1 Corinthians 10:13)

I find this very comforting; don't you?

- Ultimately, God has a plan. You may not have a plan, you may have had a plan but it did not materialise; you may have messed up your plan or you may now be on plan a, b, c... it does not matter because God always has a plan. We know from Jeremiah that He wants to bring us an 'expected end'. It means God has an expectation for everyone and He Himself will bring us there.

"… Eye hath not seen, nor ear heard, neither have
entered into the heart of man, the things which God
hath prepared for them that love Him"

(1 Corinthians 2:9).

Isn't God amazing! It means, no matter the plan you
have for yourself, it is still not compared to the plan
God Himself has for you. So many of us wonder
why our plans seem not to work out at times. That
is because if they are not in line with God's plans
then they are indeed a lost cause. Albeit, you can
still make plans and prepare if you can, but always
plan with God in mind, knowing that God will not
want evil to befall you and will not have any glory in
your failure. He only wants to be part of your plans,
and wants you to learn to trust and rely on Him and
Him alone.

*"The horse is prepared against the day of battle;
but safety is the Lord."*

(Proverbs 21:31)

God wants us to exercise patience. Lack of patience is one
of the greatest hindrances to a complete breakthrough and
testimony. We make hasty decisions in our moments of
pressure; we jump to costly conclusions in our weak moments
and most of all we prematurely demand a harvest of miracles
when we have not taken time to sow. Patience must run its
full course. I must say I am still learning this myself.

There are different aspects to a person's identity. There
is your identity at home, at work, at church, amongst your

friends, amongst those who do not hold the same faith as you, in private, or online. You can identify with several roles and still be at one with yourself.

The problem arises when you wear many hats and still feel unconnected, or you have so many 'identities' but cannot identify who you really are.

Let me give you an example. I am naturally an outspoken person, I like to talk, mingle and meet new people. When I am at home I tend not talk as much as people think but I am completely myself. When I am at work, I am not completely myself, I have to 'curb' my enthusiasm about my faith to an extent so as not to be offensive to some. I am mostly myself when I am at church, considering I am a leader, but very conservative in public. When I am online, I am not as vocal, just observant. You can say I tend to adjust to my environment without losing who I am.

It is very important to be able to 'adjust' when necessary, to your environment without losing who you are. You can be accommodating of others views and opinions without compromising your own views and faith. Of course, learn from others and identify any room for change and improvement but do so, again without losing your identity in Christ.

Growing Pains

I was very insecure as a teenager, and I did not really know why anyone would want to be my friend. Due to this I settled for less. I did not expect much from friends even though it felt like I gave a lot. I did not necessarily have a 'best friend' – you know that one person who just wanted to hang out with you, well that is how it felt to me anyway. I grew somewhat out of it a little and turned that feeling into a 'it's their loss' attitude. I figured if I meant something to someone then I would not have to try so hard to be their friend.

I started enjoying my own company. The way to do this is to find what you are good at, what you actually enjoy, and be interested in your own self. Be creative, you cannot be good company to others if you have not been good company to yourself. I found my need for company and friends all the time was hindering my own productivity. When I am fulfilled in myself, I always have a lot to offer others and then they are more likely to want to be around me.

I found it is very important to analyse who I am before others analyse me. Do not be afraid to look 'into' yourself. You will be surprised what you will discover. It means, you will not always need the validation of 'cool people' to feel cool. I remember acknowledging within myself that I am who I am – a Christian African girl with an unconventional family, who is confident and loves to sing. In those days this was all I knew. I had to accept it before I could build on it. I used to wish I was born to Michael Jackson! When reality set in that I could not change certain things about myself, I decided to use it to my advantage. It meant I had a story to tell.

Whilst at secondary school in Ireland I joined a talent show. I was, if not the only black girl on the show that year, one of the few. I joined the school choir. In an Irish school, I wanted to make a difference. My picture may still be on the wall of the school till today for being a part of the show for two years. I decided to write an article to be part of the yearbook for two years. I made the decision to be 'known' for being brave, because I did not want to be known just for being the 'odd one out'.

Youthful Adventures

Even though I was still 'finding myself' like most people my age, I had learnt something vital. I learnt, 'my difference is my advantage' so what I see as a 'lack' is only fuel for success. With this realisation and, of course, the encouragement of God I was able to embrace unfamiliar territories and attempt new things.

I remember how I got one of my first jobs at 16. I was walking along a small-town centre and noticed an advert for a 'junior stylist' at an Irish hair salon. I had never been a hairstylist, had no experience in such a setting, and definitely had no exposure to any other hair texture except the African hair. I applied for the job. I clearly remember asking myself if I knew what I was doing by applying to work there.

I decided I had nothing to lose, as it would either be a yes or a no. To my surprise I secured the job. I was the only black person there, in fact no black person came in there to do their hair. I emphasise this because it was completely outside my comfort zone, it was not synonymous with my 'identity' but that did not deter me at all. I worked hard, and became popular for giving the best hair wash. You see my mum had always taught me to use all 10 fingers when washing hair, she would tell me to really dig deep into the scalp and massage it and give the hair a good rinse, because of the nature of our hair.

This 'difference' and background gave me my advantage. I would take the time on the client's hair, and without fake nails I was able to really 'get' to where a soothing touch is needed most. Oh, how the clients appreciated the 'difference'. Soon I started getting tips just for washing hair! I was not trained to cut or style hair, but I could give a good wash. So here I was in a new territory having an experience I will never forget as an African 16-year-old in an all-white Irish salon. I flourished, and even when I had to leave due to relocation, I was given a glowing recommendation letter, a send-off and gifts.

From this one experience as a 16-year-old with a complicated life, low self-esteem but a zest for life, I decided, not to just be different, (others could see I was already different), but I decided to use my difference to teach others about tolerance and culture. The power is in your decision. You can choose to use your experience, culture, education, imperfections, as a limitation of who you are or as a strengthening factor in who you can become or are destined to be.

Never forget you are the main actor in the movie of your life. If you let Him in, God will be the executive producer and the Holy Spirit your director in Chief. Ever notice how actors are offered more challenging roles when they have done well in a previously challenging role? Or how they get their peculiar 'identity' as actors because of their attitude to taking risks and new challenges.

Take Jackie Chan, for example; he is one of the world's most renowned martial artists, he became better and more famous the more daring stunts he performed. He is also a singer (another identity), but most people know him for his daring stunts.

Likewise, you are a main actor and player in your 'life's movie', if you don't dare to do new things and embrace new challenges, you may miss out on a 'blockbuster life'.

This is perhaps why many people would rather sit and watch 'reality tv' these days or watch vlogs of people living their lives whilst yours is just 'ordinary; you don't feel like your life is worth watching, you are making your 'life's movie' boring by not participating in your own life and letting society dictate your identity and sense of worth.

As you read this, I want you to know there are hidden talents and seeds of greatness within you. How do I know? From these scriptures below, I am very convinced that every one of us: great, small, whoever, whatever and from wherever, is a masterpiece of God's creation. God is so great; nothing can get past Him; yet He is so close that He knows us all in detail. Nothing about you is insignificant to Him; He made you and loves you just the way you are. Your imperfections are just like a work of art, and only the Chief Architect understands why they are there.

This is what God says about you and me:

"Eye has not seen, nor ear heard, nor have entered into the heart of man, the things which God has prepared for those who love Him."

(1 Corinthians 2:9)

"Before I formed you in the womb, I knew you, and before you were born, I consecrated you; I appointed you a prophet to the nations."

(Jeremiah 1:5)

"... He ... set me apart before I was born,
and called me by His grace..."

(Galatians 1:15)

Choir Director

I have always loved to sing. It's another way to express myself and show how I really feel. It's not that I would put myself in the same category of renowned singers out there but I am a singer in my own right. I did not struggle as such in discovering this part of my identity. To be a singer, you must be bold, and not afraid of singing in front of people. This means you have to take the risk of ridicule or praise, since either reaction from people can lead to loss of confidence or overconfidence; it's a risk I take all the time. My love of singing and being heard supersedes the fear of ridicule I suppose. Sometimes I don't get it right, but I keep trying. Making a living out of music is not my aim. I want to make an impact through singing, whether it is to the man on the street or the masses.

As a kid, I loved dancing, I still do. My grandma always told me I had a special love for music as a child that I would dance in front of the neighbours and old folks when the music was played aloud in our community. She would tell me, I did not care who was watching and would dance away to old folk music. Music provided a way of 'escape' for my soul to express itself. As a result, I yearned to share my 'freedom' with others through singing.

I was initially shy of singing in front of people. Believe it or not, I was terrified of what they will would say and think of me. What made me change? Well, I cannot really put a finger on it. I suppose it was just the understanding, I am gifted by God and want to share that gift with others regardless of their perception of me. I figured people would love or hate me regardless of what I did, so I might as well do it for me and most importantly for God. I learnt, people mostly do not like what they cannot understand or accept what they are not 'part of'. The best way to overcome shyness is to also think of yourself with humility as 'nothing' and in the same sense, think of yourself as 'something' in terms of being God's child.

Back home in Nigeria when I was in a boarding secondary school, I decided never again to be shy of singing in front of people. In those days the student leaders would always ask us in church, 'does anyone have a 'special number'?' I remember seeing various singers and groups give their 'special number'. A special number request is just another way of asking if anyone wanted to sing (like asking anyone in a pub to sing karaoke).

This was how I started singing in my church in Leicester, UK. I was still new to the church. I did not feel the need to join the choir at the time, and just content with attending service and getting to know people because it was a very different setting to what I was used to. One day, the pastor's wife randomly asked the congregation if anyone has a 'special number'. My hand shot up! I remember singing 'the battle belongs to the Lord' by Jamie Owens-Collins.

Perhaps she was led to ask because it is not a normal practice here and it has never been asked in that manner since then. From that faithful Sunday, I have not stopped singing. Who would have known, a simple opportunity to sing would become a great stepping stone in my ministry?

From then I joined the church choir, joined another local choir that had the honour of singing for the Queen of England! I sang for an East Midland Sports awards ceremony, for ITV during a Christmas programme on BBC radio. I became a choir director at 20 years old. I had the privilege of teaching others music and loved the occasions of ministering as a form of outreach. After meeting my husband, I discovered my love for song writing also. At the time, he was just a friend who had just joined the church as a keyboardist.

We had a convention where a guest preacher was visiting. As part of the preparations, I met with him to rehearse a solo song for the event. As practice went on, we became carried away and started making up a brand-new song. It was so exciting, we decided that one day we would write and make music together. Well, the rest – as they say – is history because, by the grace of God, we have since written and produced many songs together, recorded some and have many more on the way!

Pastor

From being a choir director, I was exposed to the need for shepherds to feed and care for God's people. There is a difference between just being a choir leader and being a shepherd. One can be both but not all are. Many choir directors are very technical, they know how to teach music and songs but cannot lead the people into fulfilling their own calling or give them a real purpose to being part of the choir. Some other choir leaders are not so technical but they are more interested in gathering people to sing for events, and they look out for the general well-being of the choristers. I would like to think that I am combination of both, not overly technical but caring for the personal well-being of the 'flock'.

I started to see the choir as a church. I would organise our own programmes, our own hall for practice outside the provisions of the main church. I cared much for the state of the choristers, may be a little more than they bargained for! I went through a lot of highs and lows. The highs of getting new members, going for events and ministering to people, singing a very great song; to the lows of disappointments, desertion, frustration, tiredness and the mother of all – betrayal by the very choir members I cared for.

Little did I know, taking the choir seriously like a church was exactly what God wanted me to do! Perhaps he saw my faithfulness with little and thought to bless me with much. My leaders and fathers in the church also thought so I believe, and they decided to send me to start a church! I was sent to Rugby town to start a branch of our church there. This was indeed scary! How did I go from being a nice, secure choir shepherd to being a church planter?

I was officially appointed to be a Lady Pastor a year and few months after planting a church. My life has not been the same ever since. I am still learning what it entails and God has been faithful and patient with me. Perhaps one day if Jesus tarries and He permits me I will be able to share in depth my experience, challenges, trials and triumphs of being a modern-day female African pastor, mother, wife and career woman.

Friends, you can see from my story that God will use you if you are not afraid to be used. God will direct you if you are willing to be led. I once heard a comment from a preacher who said, we often ask God to use us but later complain to God we feel used; we ask God to make us a bridge to Him and later moan to God that people are walking all over us. This indeed is a true reflection of how quickly we forget our covenant with God and our destiny. How you start your journey is not the destination, but it will form part of your experience if you can embrace it and see God's hand in the grand scheme of events.

The road to identifying your true self and purpose may seem long and patchy but God wants you to trust Him. He ultimately wants the best for you as Jeremiah 29:11 tells us. Even if you don't know what you are doing, trust God – the One who knows what He is doing with you. He will come through and true for you.

So, who am I in Christ?

By the grace of God, I am a Child of God, Daughter of the Most High God, sanctified and set apart as a vessel unto honour. I am blessed to be a Song writer, Singer, Choir coach, Author, Teacher, Preacher, Church planter and whoever or whatever God wants me to be for the sake of the gospel. I intend on utilising all to the best of my abilities, so help me God.

I join with the apostle Paul in affirming:

> "… by the grace of God, I am what I am, and His grace towards me was not in vain: but I laboured more abundantly than they all, yet not I, but the grace of God which was with me."
>
> *(1 Corinthians 15:10)*

"… but you are a chosen generation, a royal priesthood,
a holy nation, His one special people, that you may
proclaim the praises of Him who called you out of
darkness into His marvellous light."

(1 Peter 2:9)

Call to Action

Ponder on some of the gifts and talents you feel God has
blessed you with, then write down what you are very good
at and what you find easy to do. What do you think? Are
you blessed or what?!

Chapter 6

Forgiveness Made Easier

Forgiveness is something most of us desire from others but find it hard to give. It takes faith to forgive and faith to receive forgiveness. We underestimate the power of forgiveness and often we abuse it. In the Bible, the Pharisees were astonished to find, not only did Jesus have the power to heal, to raise the dead and to do many wonders, He also had the power to forgive. Their reaction and indignation following Jesus's declaration suggests, the power to forgive was not common to humans. Therefore, they accused Him of blasphemy.

Today we live in a culture where unforgiveness is thriving. We are quick to judge, point fingers, report, pick on faults and complain. In fact, there are many careers built specifically to do these things. This is because as humans we have become distrustful and impatient and have not fully embraced the importance of forgiveness. The grace to forgive is not very common. Very few people ask God for grace to be able to forgive daily just as He forgives us daily.

The truth is we have a problem of letting go; it is far easier to hold on to a hurt than to let go. By default, we are unforgiving, and forgiveness is just not natural to us. In *Genesis 4:1-9,* we learn that Cain killed his brother Abel. The conversation between God and Cain seemed to suggest, Cain may have killed his brother for many reasons such as jealousy, bitterness, anger or indeed because of his un-forgiveness towards God and his brother. I believe it is as a result of this inherent weakness of man not to let go of issues, **that God used our forgiveness of one another as a condition for Him to forgive us.** We are ultimately given the choice and the freewill to live or be forever condemned in our sin without hope of forgiveness and redemption.

> *"... but if you do not forgive men their trespasses,*
> *neither will your Father forgive your trespasses."*
>
> *(Matthew 6:15)*

God knows how destructive un-forgiveness is. In His wisdom, He will sometimes allow us to go through humbling experiences in life to make us value forgiveness. Sadly, our hearts can be hardened at times so instead of forgiving one another, we are bent on having our own way – all in the name of revenge.

Jesus told of an interesting, insightful parable of two servants.

"Therefore, the kingdom of heaven is like a certain king who wanted to settle accounts with his servants. And when he had begun to settle accounts, one was brought to him who owed him ten thousand talents. But as he was not able to pay, his master commanded that he be sold, with his wife and children and all that he had, and that payment be made. The servant therefore fell down before him, saying, 'Master, have patience with me, and I will pay you all. Then the master of that servant was moved with compassion, released him, and forgave him the debt. But that servant went out and found one of his fellow servants who owed him a hundred denarii; and he laid hands on him and took him by the throat, saying, 'Pay me what you owe!' So, his fellow servant fell down at his feet and begged him, saying, 'Have patience with me, and I will pay you all.' And he would not, but went and threw him into prison till he should pay the debt. So, when his fellow servants saw what had been done, they were very grieved, and came and told their master all that had been done. Then his master, after he had called him, said to him, 'You wicked servant! I forgave you all that debt because you begged me. Should you not also have had compassion on your fellow servant, just as I had pity on you?' And his master was angry, and delivered him to the torturers until he should pay all that was due to him. So, my heavenly Father also will do to you if each of you, from his heart, does not forgive his brother his trespasses."

(Matthew 18:21-35)

Revenge is bitter-sweet

I have often been asked; what if I cannot forgive? What if I find it difficult to let go, especially since the person who hurt me will not admit they have done wrong? What if I want them to also feel pain and sorrow just as they made me feel? Does that make me a bad person?

First of all, it is perfectly normal and humane to feel this way. It just shows that forgiveness is not as simple and easy as it seems sometimes. Let's address each of the questions:

- **What if I cannot forgive?** – the key word here is 'cannot'. I would ask 'why not'? Think carefully about yourself and the reasons why you feel you cannot forgive someone. Hopefully, looking within yourself will help identify your own shortcomings. Remember try not to let 'pride' and 'victimhood' hinder you from true freedom. Ask yourself, would you want to be forgiven if you were to do something wrong? Also, its ok to ask God for help to forgive. It is possible you will find the strength and grace to let go. Trust the process.
- **What if I find it difficult to let go, especially since the person who hurt me will not admit they have done wrong?** – Admittedly, this is one of the main reasons why we find it difficult to forgive i.e. When others seem to have 'gotten-away' with doing you wrong. Think about your ' circle of influence', try not to be frustrated and worried about what is outside of your control. You cannot control what others do and don't do. As much as you wish they will realise their

mistake and come to you for forgiveness, accept and understand that it may never happen. We are complex beings, pride and self-righteousness may be a factor hindering reconciliation. Focus on your healing, your journey, your successes not on the other person. Remember your need for peace and healing supersedes their pride.

- **What if I want them to also feel pain and sorrow just as they made me feel? Does that make me a bad person?** – This is the main reason why some action movies are so popular! It is mostly based on revenge. To seek revenge or some compensation is perfectly normal, only that sometimes it is misplaced. I always say that the person who can truly revenge evil is God. He is the best 'Defender' of all. Allow God to fight your battles and revenge on your behalf. He knows more about the situation than you do, so let Him put things right in the way you cannot.

…And the LORD said to him, 'Therefore, whoever kills Cain, **vengeance shall be taken on him sevenfold**. And the Lord set a mark on Cain, lest anyone finding him should kill him'…

(Genesis 4:15NKJV)

…Dear friends, never take revenge. Leave that to the righteous anger of God. For the Scriptures say, "**I will take revenge; I will pay them back**", says the Lord.

(Romans 12:19 NLT)

Reasons why we should forgive

1. **Forgiveness brings healing and deliverance**. Never forget, only God can truly deliver us from sin through forgiveness. It liberates the offender, providing justification – 'Just as if' you never offended – for the offence and empowers the offended.

People were astonished when Jesus said *"your sins are forgiven"* (Luke 7:28) Up until then, no-one had the power or boldness to forgive offences, and the main ethos was 'an eye for an eye'. But Jesus came to not only demonstrate the Power of God to heal the sick, raise the dead, walk on water, open blind eyes but He came to also show the power of forgiveness!

Many of us are eager to learn from Jesus in terms of how He prayed on the mountains, how He preached in the synagogues, how He rebuked the devils, how He selected His disciples, how He dealt with religious leaders and more, but we often overlook how He forgave those who did Him wrong!

You see, the very presence of Jesus walking the earth, is a demonstration of the Fathers forgiveness and compassion towards us. Jesus walked the earth in the flesh; therefore, He experienced rejection, abuse, hatred, pain, sorrow and injustice at the hands of humanity. He also experienced the greatest pain of all, when He bore the sins of the world and had to be rejected by the Father on the Cross.

"… and at the ninth hour Jesus cried out with a loud voice, saying: 'Eloi, Eloi, lama sabachthani?' which is translated, 'My God, My God, why have You forsaken me?'"

(Mark 15:34)

- Jesus exhibited the highest act of forgiveness when He:

  Decided to call on the Father even though He felt rejected when His Father turned His face away.

- Continuing to obey the Father by remaining on the cross till our redemption was accomplished when he said 'It is finished'.

- He looked on from the cross to his offenders, his persecutors and murderers through the eyes of love and grace and He summed up all the foolishness and accorded it to mere ignorance:

> "Then Jesus said, 'Father, forgive them, for they do not know what they do.' and they divided His garments and cast lots."
>
> *(Luke 23:34)*

Many of us would have felt justified to 'quit' on the cross. We would have jumped off the cross and reminded God how hard we tried to make it work. Many of us would have duly seen to it that each one of our persecutors and mockers get exactly what they deserve. Yet Jesus demonstrated great grace in forgiveness, and though tempted at all points, He restrained Himself on the Cross and implored the Father to forgive us whilst still bearing our pain.

2.   God shows us mercy, patience and compassion on a daily basis. We are therefore, also required to show the same for our fellow beings, if we are ever to be offered forgiveness by God. Without Gods' forgiveness, we can never be free of the payment for our trespasses and we would have to bear the weight of guilt forever. However, receiving God's forgiveness means total freedom from guilt and shame, freedom from eternal condemnation and doom.

Aside from Jesus, who is the express image of Almighty God, Our God is also an excellent example for of forgiveness and how to forgive others, we must learn and emulate His attribute of long suffering.

It is easy for me to forgive the reckless driver who swore at me in a road rage. Why? Because it is highly likely that I will never ever meet that driver again and it only happened once. For most of us it is easy to let go in that situation. The real challenge comes when you have to face prolonged offence and suffering as a result of someone's actions or decisions. How do we lay down our pride and 'right' to begrudge that person forever? Well, we can only turn to God. Just as we turn to Him for situations beyond our control, we must also look to God to help us 'suffer long' whilst remaining gracious enough to forgive.

Ultimately, we determine whether God should forgive us by whether or not we forgive others. God is watching if you will forgive others so He can also forgive you. The power to executive judgement on our offenders can be a great temptation. Like any other quest for power, if not handled correctly, it will lead to self-destruction.

Sometimes there seem to be no apparent reason why we should forgive someone who has so inhumanly treated us. Why should I forgive? 'I have a right to bear this grudge and nurse the hurt' I hear someone say. Well, I agree, unforgiveness may seem like the only power we have to control those who have wronged us. I agree, it is bitter to be the wounded party; it is also sweet to inflict the same pain experienced on others especially on the offender. However, in the end it leaves a sour taste.

Unforgiveness, it is just like any other sin, sweet at first but deadly at the end, bearing many consequences. Therefore, when all is said and done, after moaning about the hurt, after coming to terms with the wrong done to you, you must decide to let go and forgive.

Someone once ascribed unforgiveness to holding gastric gases within the bowels. Those around you are oblivious to the pain and harmful substances you are holding in. You may feel ashamed to let go or feel you need to protect those around you by holding it all in. You will be the one feeling the discomfort and aches within you. However, you need to let go. Once you decide to let go, you will experience a huge relief! Remember, your need to forgive must be more than their need for forgiveness. Once all bitterness and unforgiveness is out, it is less harmful to you.

- Forgive others because to be unforgiving and unforgiven is to be in a perpetual state of darkness. God's Light and Presence cannot be in our lives where sin is unconfessed and unforgiven. (2 Corinthians 2:5-11)
- Forgive for the sake of Christ. I once heard an Easter message entitled 'Christ is risen, we are forgiven, and we must forgive'.

"Therefore, as the elect of God, holy and beloved,

Put on tender mercies, kindness, humility, meekness,

longsuffering; bearing with one another, and forgiving one

another, if anyone has a complaint against another; even as

Christ forgave you, so you also must do. But above all these

things put on love, which is the bond of perfection. And

let the peace of God rule in your hearts, to which also you

were called in one body; and be thankful.

Let the word of Christ dwell in you richly in all wisdom,

teaching and admonishing one another in also you were

called in one body; and be thankful.

Let the word of Christ dwell in you richly in all wisdom,

teaching and admonishing one another in psalms and

hymns and spiritual songs, singing with grace in your

hearts to the Lord. And whatever you do in word or

deed, do all in the name of the Lord Jesus, giving thanks

to God the Father through Him.'"

(Colossians 3:12-17)

We are asked to **put on** these things because it takes a conscious effort to exhibit them. They are not qualities we are naturally born with so we have to cultivate it by applying God's Word and by the help of the Holy Spirit.

Paul understood, there will indeed be quarrels and disputes and offence just as Jesus pre-warned. After all we are humans who err. However, he encourages us to forgive one another. Although it is not easy to do, we must forgive because Christ forgave us!! And it will take an ungrateful, forgetful person to forget what Christ did and so not forgive others.

3.   Another reason for forgiveness is so we can exhibit love, grace, faithfulness and justice just like our Heavenly Father who embodies these attributes in manifold greatness.

> "This is the message which we have heard from Him and declare to you, that God is light and in Him is no darkness at all."
>
> *(1 John 1:5-10)*

Another key ingredient which lies with the offender is confession. To confess our sins is to admit them, renounce them and repent from them. When we do this, coupled with forgiving others, God will do His part to forgive us.

When we have done wrong to others, it is good practice to confess our sins, admit our wrong and make amends so the offended party will be encouraged by you to also forgive easily. The cycle of forgiveness continues.

When we neglect to pray for each other, offences become highly inevitable. Satan gets the opportunity to tempt us into doing wrong against our brethren. Offence is what leads to hurt, hurt amounts to unforgiveness and unforgiveness leads to eternal damnation.

> "… for if you forgive others their sins, your heavenly Father will also forgive you. But if you do not forgive others, your Father will not forgive you your sins."
>
> *(Matthew 6:14-15).*

Therefore, the enemy will persist in making us a stumbling block to one another and ourselves through offences.

When Jesus was about to be betrayed, beaten and crucified, He warned His disciples beforehand. He had told them to be prayerful and to be watchful. He predicted how Peter would deny Him and how the others would run away. Perhaps if Jesus's disciples had prayed enough for one another, then Satan may not have tempted Judas to betray Christ. Perhaps if Peter had prayed for himself after Christ warned him of what would happen, then he may have overcome the temptation to deny Christ. We must pray for one another and for ourselves because the probability of being offended and offending is high, the temptation to harbour unforgiveness is strong and the consequence of unforgiveness is dire. Frankly, the price for not forgiving yourself or another person is just too high.

Forgiveness Made Easy

One of the many things Jesus did on the Cross for us was to make forgiveness easy. Without Jesus's sacrifice, our sins would remain unforgiven, meaning eternal damnation would be sure.

> "… then Jesus said, 'Father, forgive them,
> for they do not know what they do."
>
> *(Luke 23:34)*

Jesus became the sacrificial lamb for the ultimate sacrifice for our sins. Because of Him we have remission of sin. Aside from Him there is no other way to receive forgiveness. Forgiveness cannot be bought or worked for. It is free because of Christ's finished work on the Cross. His obedience to do Gods Will. We must never take this for granted.

To be forgiven by God is truly a blessing. How amazing it is for such a pure God to love an impure people like us enough to forgive our sins and forget it!!

We cannot hide our sins from God, so to receive true forgiveness we have to truly repent and be honest with ourselves. God sees the heart and knows what evil is hidden within it. However, the act of confessing our sin and repenting is actually for us to acknowledge our ways before God. We do it for our children all the time. Confession helps us to understand, what we have done is punishable and so we need to ask God to exercise His mercy. This way we develop a repentant heart not just a show of repentance.

Points to bear in mind about forgiveness:

- Always remember, you reap what you sow. Sowing forgiveness reaps forgiveness. Caution is necessary here. It is possible to be forgiving towards other people, but still others seem to find it difficult to forgive you. It does not mean, you are not doing the right thing to forgive an unforgiving person, or you should feel cheated; it just means, you look to God alone to reap the forgiveness you have sown. It is so easy to look for an immediate reward, to immediately demand reciprocity. That could prove futile and frustrating. Forgive, not because you will reap the same from the people who hurt you. It is of course ideal to receive the same in return; but do not focus on others, look to God who will reward your faith and obedience Himself. He will show you the kindness you've shown others and duly recompense your efforts towards others. (Luke 6:37-42)

- Always consider yourself. Before reacting to an action or before passing judgement on an offence to you, please stop and think of yourself. Think of your human frailties and weakness as opposed to what that person has done to you, as this may lead to self-righteousness. But by comparison, let us strive to compare our actions to Jesus, our ultimate example of perfection.

We should not compare ourselves to other people because all have sinned and come short of the glory of God. Jesus is our righteousness, and there is no sin in Him. He walked the earth like you and me and was subjected to the same temptations like you and me (Lust of the eyes, Lust of the flesh, Pride of Life – 1 John 2:16) and yet did not sin. This makes Him qualified to be titled the 'perfect man'. He was not tempted as a heavenly being or as the Son of God. He was tempted as a man, at His lowest point, as a man.

"… and why do you look at the speck in your brother's eye, but do not consider the plank in your own eye?"

(Matthew 7:3)

So, we have to consider ourselves in order to be merciful to others. Analyse the offender, analyse the offence, analyse the situation. Understand, you may have made the same error in judgement, should the circumstances be reversed if you had been in the offender's shoes.

- Remember, forgiving the offender does not necessarily mean forgetting the offence or the hurt. Forgiving does not also mean you forget the feeling associated with the offence and forget about your offenders. We often equate forgetting about something to forgiving. It is possible to forgive others but you still remember very much what they did. However, the key is not to let the memory of the past control your present or hold your future to ransom. It is very difficult to forget sins, offences and transgressions committed against you and it is impossible without Gods help. (Psalm 25:1-22)

Thanks be to God that He forgives and forgets (blots it out), else we would not be confident enough to approach Him. That's the wonderful part of Gods' forgiveness – He wipes the slate clean, no scores kept, no scores to settle, price paid with Jesus's blood, nothing owed. Interestingly enough, we are rather the ones who actually 'remind' God of our past after we have been forgiven; we allow the enemy to pull up our past records against us and let his accusations deter us from approaching the Throne of God with boldness and grace.

To forget does not necessarily mean to completely fail to recollect the offence. Whilst it is possible to completely forget, and have every trace of the wrong doing erased from your memory, that is indeed a miracle. It is a miracle, I pray for myself. 'Forgetting' means, you don't have the incident or situation constantly in the forefront of your mind, and your mind does not dwell on it as it used to do when it happened, or you are no longer feeling the pain associated with the memory of being hurt. I must admit, it is only by the grace of God that I have been able to 'forgive and forget the hurt caused by those who betrayed me. I am still 'forgetting'. It is said, time heals all wounds, and time has aided in forgetting some of the things that offended me.

Through God I remember less, do not dwell on the situation and am able to talk about the experience without the initial sting of hurt and bitterness I felt.

It is important to note it is sometimes good for us to remember what we went through, though we may have forgiven. This is so we can remain humble, continue to rely on God for strength and so we can be in a better position to share our experiences with others and indeed learn from our mistakes.

- Never forget that God also has an interest in pardoning our sins, no matter how great they are. He asks for a repentant heart and the willingness to change our ways.

"Say to them: 'As I live,' says the Lord God, 'I have no pleasure in the death of the wicked, but that the wicked turn from his way and live. Turn, turn from your evil ways! For why should you die, O house of Israel?'"

(Ezekiel 33:11)

He forgives us for His Name's sake and places our sins into the sea of forgetfulness. (Acts 13:38-43)

As mentioned before, when God forgives and pardons our sins we are not only forgiven, we are also 'Justified' – just as if we never did it. It is however important, we always remember and believe this promise of God in order to be truly free.

May God give us the grace to forgive and forget every hurt.

Lord's Prayer test

The best way to know, you have forgiven someone is the 'freedom' to pray for them.

There is the Lord's Prayer test, I learnt from my Pastor Dag Heward Mills. In essence he challenges that we can test if truly forgiveness is taking place in our heart, if we are able to insert the name of the offender in the Lords' prayer without feeling animosity towards that person. To illustrate:

> Our Father who is in Heaven,
> Hallowed be your Name
> Your Kingdom come,
> Your Will be done on earth as it is in Heaven
> Give us this day our daily bread
> Forgive us our trespasses
> Even as I forgive ... *Insert Name*
> Deliver us from evil
> For thine is the Kingdom, Your Power and Glory
> Forever and ever Amen.

Call to Action

- Write down or say out loud a particular painful experience, you feel you may not have forgiven or the memory is still very vivid and painful.
- Pray for those who hurt you by inserting their names into 'The Lord's Prayer' as illustrated above.

Talk out loud to God and tell Him how it feels, and allow yourself to be comforted by God.

Your Heavenly Father loves you dearly, and He wants to keep you safe and away from pain. He will convert the pain you feel right now into praise.

He says 'Sorry, I know how you feel and it will get better'.

Chapter 7

Victor or Victim?

There is the saying, your view point depends on your point of view. What's more, with the correct pedestal and the right lens, your view point can be clearer and extend even further.

This chapter is about viewing life's situations through God's eyes, though still feeling the pain as a human being. It will show you how you can make the decision to turn life's unfavourable situations and experiences into a victorious testimony of how you overcame.

No doubt everyone has experienced, is currently experiencing and will experience some challenges in life. These experiences make us who we are, and give us something to talk about, cry about, laugh about, moan about and more.

It is quite interesting to note, no one has a 'unique' or exclusive life experience/challenge. Indeed, As observed by King Solomon,

"That which has been is what will be, that which is
done is what will be done, and there is nothing new
under the sun."

(Ecclesiastes 1:9)

Someone somewhere, has been through what you are going through or what you went through. However, the unique thing about what we go through is that no two persons will come to the same conclusions from the same experience. Though two people may have experienced betrayal in marriage, they will each interpret their experiences in a different way or 'view' it in a different way. That is, they will either forever view that experience from the point of view as a victim of circumstance or a victor over life's challenges.

I have come to understand, a person will choose to live as a victim or victor depending on what their natural disposition is. Each individual has different natural tendencies, strengths, weaknesses, different background, sensitivity levels, threshold for pain, and endurance level. Therefore, how each individual views a situation can be dependent on a mixture of variables.

This means it is possible for a person to be more affected psychologically than another person who faced the same situation. Therefore understand, anyone can be a victim of something or someone but not everyone can be a victor. No one chooses to be a victim, but one can choose to be a victor. You ask – 'how is it possible to decide to be a victor and not a victim?' Well, although it is certainly not an easy thing to do, it is possible. When you have been wronged in life, it is easy to cling to the fleeting comforts of victimhood, people feeling sorry for you, helping you to fight the wrong doer or echoing your own thoughts of despair.

It is easy to just keep regurgitating the hurt and pain you feel always, not as a testimony but as a test you never fully overcame. People will do their best to sympathise with you and even express holy anger at the perpetrator. But when all is said and done, though they mean well, they can never truly alleviate the burden of the horrible experience you are going through. The best they can do to really be of help is to pray for you.

When I found out about my husband's infidelity, I did not react as you would see in the movies or as you would expect a person in my position to react. Though I had my moments of weakness where there was some resentment and disgust, I never actually 'cussed anyone out' or anything of that sort. I would see the other women in church, on my street, even some who till this day don't know, I know they had slept with my husband. It was all I could do to keep what was left of my dignity.

At some point I did feel the need to confront all of these women and tell them just how evil they had behaved but I did not. I held my peace knowing for sure, the Holy Spirit is much better at convicting and executing judgement than I ever could.

There is a battle between my flesh and the Spirit of God in me as to how I react when I remember my perpetrators. In every sense of the word, I leave them to God.

You cannot live life to the full when you hold on to the passing comfort of being a victim. Decide to be a victor, overcome the challenges of your experience by using it as a catalyst for positive change on your outlook on life.

Things happen in life, you are not the first, and you will not be the last. Life is too short to keep playing the victim card. Yes, you do not deserve such an act of betrayal but the betrayer has the burden of living with their actions for the rest of their lives even when they have found peace in God.

Just look at what happened to Judas. He could not bear to live with his actions and took his own life as a result. I am not saying all the perpetrators in your life will end up resorting to suicide because of what they did to you. I am only stating that the evil that people do lives after them. Peter, on the other hand, reacted differently. Though he was both a victim of accusation and a betrayer, he chose to be a victor and overcame the burden of guilt and shame to then become a great Apostle and Father of the church.

People are watching you, and looking out for your reaction or lack of it. Everything you do is a message to someone. When word got out, my husband had affairs, many people at our church, didn't even know how to act around me. Some were awkward and ashamed to even look me in the eye and be genuine. In times of trouble, expect people around you, may not acknowledge your struggles or offer a word of encouragement, prayer or comfort. Expect, some may even believe you deserve every bad thing that happens to you. Others are entitled to their opinions about you, but no one else can be 'you'. Therefore, it is ok to let people be who they are. There is a funny phrase: 'people are not people but people will always be people', it is a mysterious oxymoron, which means although people can be very evil, like the devil himself, they are still only human with frailties.

You must get to the point where you really dig deep in God and look only to God for your sense of worth. Do not let people's opinions about you get to you, especially if this does not develop the fruits of the Spirit in you. The fruits of the Spirit are love, joy, peace, long-suffering, kindness, goodness, faithfulness, gentleness and self-control. I have come to accept, sometimes even well-meaning people can say the wrong things at the wrong time. Therefore, we must learn to 'filter' through what people say, good and/or bad, get what is meaningful to your soul and spirit then move on. Always filter out these unhelpful voices and pay attention to the corresponding voice of the Holy Spirit who is really the only One who knows where it hurts and how to fix it.

Deciding to be a victor may take some element of control out of your hands. You see God cannot be of much comfort to you if you have found comfort in your misery and reliance on others. You have to let go and let God. In the same vein, those who care for you may not be able to comfort you effectively if you are determined to remain miserable and victimised. I made a very calculated, conscious effort to not let all I have been through and still going through determine my outlook in life.

No, I refuse such a curse, and you must do too. Do not let the devil rob you of the blessed assurance that Jesus is yours and will never leave you! And if He be for us who can be against us. He never promised a stress-free life or a pain free life. In our weakness He is made strong in us, and because He is strong, we can find strength to carry on. Jesus received 'promotion' *(Philippians 2:10)*, because He persevered through His pain to go through the betrayal of men and the shame of The Cross. He became a Victor for us all. He is our example. We must also draw strength and courage from His experience and do the same, not in our own way or in our own strength, but through Christ who strengthens us.

Challenges form character

There is another saying: 'what does not kill you will make you stronger'. This is true only if you don't die emotionally. Many survive challenges in life but are left permanently damaged emotionally and mentally. It is hard to tell when someone is suffering emotionally, but there are now various diagnosis[1] for various emotional and mental traumas such as anxiety disorders, social anxiety, panic attacks, depression.

Before experiencing betrayal, I often wondered why people would call off sick at work due to 'depression', 'stress' or anxiety. I never understood the emotional pain that could be felt physically until I was in the same situation.

Naturally we are strong beings emotionally. God made us in His image so we were created to be emotionally stable beings. However, since the fall of man into sin, the dynamics changed. The world became a game of 'survival of the fittest'. Those who are fit physically, spiritually, financially, academically, emotionally, and mentally had the chance of living a fulfilled life. In all of these areas there is a test for everyone to see who is 'fit' and who can overcome the challenges to receive the glory.

In a boxing contest, the fittest is always backed to win. At a job interview, the candidate who is deemed to 'fit' the most gets the job. In an endurance test, the most mentally stable person scores higher. In the jungle the fittest animal survives. These are just few examples of how the world sees things and quite frankly we all see things this way most times.

Thankfully God does not see things the way the world sees things. But God:

> "… has chosen the foolish things of the world to put to shame the wise, and God has chosen the weak things of the world to put to shame the things which are might."
>
> *(1 Corinthians 1:27)*

Solomon said:

> "I returned and saw under the sun that— the race is not to the swift, nor the battle to the strong, nor bread to the wise, nor riches to men of understanding, nor favour to men of skill; but time and chance happen to them all."
>
> *(Ecclesiastes 9:11)*

It means, even though you lost your limbs in an accident, you can still win an Olympic race. Even if you are divorced, you can still find happiness and fulfilment. Though you were a victim of rape, you can still be a victorious ambassador of hope!

Your circumstances should not define you but should be used as contributory factors to your character if properly applied and processed. There are many instances in the Bible where people have been identified simply by their circumstances such as Simon the leper, Rahab the harlot, the woman with the issue of blood, blind Bartimaeus, Mary

Magdalene who had seven demons cast out of her, the mad man of Gadara.

Notice, it is nothing new to be called what you went through. That is life. That is the way people may choose to describe you but that should not be the way you should choose to be remembered for the rest of your life. You may call me 'Samira, the woman whose husband cheated on her' but that is not my destination, it was simply part of my journey into 'becoming' Samira. How your story ends is ultimately in God's hands but you can decide how you want it to end.

All the people mentioned above had their story changed, they refused to remain defined by their circumstances. They decided to be victors in their own right by doing everything they could to meet the destiny changer, JESUS.

> "My brethren, count it all joy when you fall into various trials, knowing that the testing of your faith produces patience. But let patience have its perfect work, that you may be perfect and complete, lacking nothing."
>
> *(James 1:2-4)*

It is important to understand, God does not purposely test us with challenges. A challenge is simply what the enemy has imposed on your character and which God uses to your advantage in order to promote you in life.

When we are set in our own ways, it is difficult to change course mid-way as we go through life. Ultimately, it is who we are and what we are made of, which determines what we get out of life. God wants us to be like Him. He wants us to be where He is. We already have something God has –

'free will'; therefore, He cannot force us to be like Him. He does not want to force us to love Him or want to be where He is. Therefore, He can only use the opportunities, which present themselves through the challenges we face.

There are many examples of this in scripture:

> In 1 Samuel 1:1-7, Hannah, wept sore to God after facing barrenness and shame from Peninah. What a humbling experience it must have been but God remembered her and blessed her with a child.
>
> In Genesis 44, Joseph's brothers had a change in character when they went through famine and ended up having to bow to the same little brother they sold to slavery.
>
> In the story of Job, we get an insight into how God uses the intentions of the devil to rather bless His children. In fact, from the story of Job it becomes clear, God is not the architect of all the diseases and pain and all sorts of loss we face. *(Job 1:1-22)* However, He uses these as an avenue to draw us closer to Him through obedience. Thinking otherwise is to accuse God of being evil and the creator of diseases and the like. God is good and all that He created is good. *"Then God looked over all he had made, and he saw that it was very good!" (Genesis 1:31).* Therefore, it is actually the devil who seeks to pollute what God has made.

God lets these things happen, not because He derives joy from watching us suffer but rather, He wants us to understand our limits. To understand where human endeavours ends, and the supernatural begins. Understand that God is relatable and because of 'free will' we have to invite Him into our situations else we will continue to use our human power, which is no match against Satan.

We are born a clean state in the sense of having no 'memorable experience'. However, most midwives can tell how your child may turn out by what they are 'experiencing in the womb'. I remember when I was pregnant with my daughter, I had attended a scan and the nurse commented, she saw my daughter yawning through the scan! It was no surprise because with every sound scan we did, I was told she was a 'very active and happy baby'. Looking at her now she fits that description perfectly. She is indeed very active and very happy. She is self-entertaining and un-reliant on people to make her happy.

As you watch your children grow, you will see how they begin to adapt to new experiences and challenges. You will begin to see a certain maturity and see their character developing. Our character runs deeper than our behaviour. Our behaviour is learnt over time and our character is built over time. I have learnt to be reserved and quiet in certain environments even though I am naturally loud and an extrovert. Some challenges I faced in life made me behave in that way. However, those same challenges have given me a 'quiet resolve' when it comes to making some of life's hard choices.

I encourage you today, do not fight the pruning; don't fight the 'Gardener' cutting away at the weeds and rough edges of your life. It is all in the grand plan of making you as beautiful and perfect as you can be on the inside as well as on the outside. Relax in God's hands as He uses the very ugly situations you face in life to make you over into the prince and princess, you really are. You are the child of a Heavenly King.

Here are some of the choices you face:

Fight or flight?

It is important to know when to stand and fight or take flight for dear life. Ultimately that choice is yours but it can be influenced by many factors.

The term 'fight-or-flight'[2] was derived from the behaviour pattern of our predecessors in terms of how they chose to deal with hostile situations or immediate dangers perceived in their environment. They could either fight or flee. Either scenario chosen prepares the body to react or respond to stress, danger and external discomfort both physiologically and psychologically.

In the 1920s the fight-or-flight response was first described and documented by American physiologist Walter Cannon. Cannon discovered that a chain of rapidly occurring reactions inside the body helped to mobilise the body's resources to deal with threatening circumstances. Today the fight-or-flight response is recognised as part of the first stage of Hans Selye's general adaptation syndrome, GAS[1] a theory describing the response to stress.

The fight-or-flight response, refers to a physiological and psychological reaction that occurs in the presence of something that is frightening or alarming, either mentally or physically. It is also known as 'the acute stress response'[2]. According to biological psychology, the response is triggered by the release of hormones that prepare your body to either stay to deal with a threat or to run away to safety.

What actually happens during a Fight-or-Flight Response?

Can you think of a time you may have experienced a fight-or-flight response?

Fight-or-flight responses can happen in the face of an imminent physical danger such as encountering a growling dog as you walk by a house or a dog walker; or it can happen as a result of a more psychological threat, for example preparing to give a major presentation at school or work.

In that moment of facing something frightening, your heartbeat would have quickened as you began to breathe faster, and your entire body would have become tense and ready to take action.

Biologically, what happens in response to acute stress is a sudden release of hormones, which activates the body's sympathetic nervous system.

Which then stimulates the adrenal glands triggering the release of catecholamines, which include adrenaline and nor-adrenaline. This results in an increase in heart rate, blood pressure, and breathing rate. After the threat is gone, it takes between 20 to 60 minutes for the body to return to its pre-arousal levels.

Physically, what happens when experiencing a fight or flight response may include:

Trembling: In the face of stress or danger, your muscles can become tense and geared up for action. This tension can result in uncontrollable trembling or shaking. It can also be as a result of the turmoil of the indecision to either fight the situation or flee from the situation, and the struggle to cope with the pressure of making that decision can lead to mental shut down.

Increased heart rate and heavy breathing: The demand for energy and oxygen increases during a time of stress or moment of danger as it is needed to fuel a rapid response to the danger. Therefore, in 'flight or fight mode', your body's respiration rate increases as well as your heartbeat.

Pale or Flushed Skin: As the stress response starts to take hold, blood flow to the surface areas of the body is reduced and flow to the muscles, brain, legs, and arms are increased. You might become pale as a result, or your face may alternate between pale and flushed as blood rushes to your head and brain, causing dizziness. The body's blood clotting ability also increases in order to prevent excess blood loss in the event of injury or fall.

Dilated Pupils: The body also prepares itself to be more aware and observant of the surroundings during times of danger. This allows more light into the eyes and results in better vision of the surroundings. You can become more sensitive to people in close proximity.

Why is it important whether we view ourselves as a victim or a victor?

The fight-or-flight response plays a critical role in how we deal with unpleasant or terrifying circumstances and the dangers we face in our lives. Essentially, at that split moment of realising the danger or threat, a choice of response is offered. Either stick around to fight what you are experiencing or decide you are not equipped enough to fight and flee from the threat. The response you choose is not a show of strength or lack of it. It is purely a decision, which requires wisdom in every given situation.

It is important to note, the response can be triggered due to both real and imaginary threats.

By preparing your body for action, you psychologically prepare yourself to be in a better position to cope under pressure. Study shows, the stress created by the situation can actually be helpful, making it more likely, you will cope effectively with the threat. This type of stress can help you perform better in situations where you are under pressure to do well, such as at work or school. In cases where the threat is life-threatening, the fight-or-flight response can actually play a critical role in your survival. By gearing you up to fight or flee, the fight-or-flight response makes it more likely, you will survive the danger.

God has naturally built in us the ability to choose how we respond to adverse situations. As mentioned above, knowing when to fight or flee is important. Scripture guides us as to what to do in any given situation:

"Therefore, take up the whole armour of God, that you may be able to withstand in the evil day, and having done all, to stand."

(Ephesians 6:13)

"Therefore, my beloved brethren, be steadfast, immovable, always abounding in the work of the Lord, knowing that your labour is not in vain in the Lord."

(1 Corinthians 15:58)

Scripture also indicates when it is not wise to fight certain desires but to run! Flee!

> "Flee sexual immorality. Every sin that a man does is outside the body, but he who commits sexual immorality sins against his own body."
>
> *(1 Corinthians 6:18)*

> "Therefore, my beloved, flee from idolatry."
>
> *(1 Corinthians 10:14)*

Understanding yourself, your strengths and your weakness, is important so you can decide on which battles to fight and which ones to leave and live to fight another day.

Through it all we must be encouraged, God is in it with us. Know that within us is the inner strength necessary for survival. It does not matter what response you chose in a terrifying situation, what matters is that you don't let the situation rule the rest of your life.

When one loses control of the power to respond to a challenging situation, it leads to things such as phobias, panic attacks and anxiety. Some of these occur as a result of responding in a fight-or-flight way even though there is no real threat. For example, you might be in a room full of people you don't know; suddenly the above physical fight-or-flight mode kicks in and you start to have a panic attack because you feel threatened that others are staring at you.

Therefore, while the fight-or-flight response happens automatically, it does not mean, it is always accurate. And even if it is accurate, understand, you have the power to overcome and to make the decision to either fight or take flight.

No matter what, decide you are a victor.

I remember the first time I found out, I might be losing my job, I actually experienced some of the above symptoms, it felt as if my heart would not stop accelerating and would constantly be in a panic mode. Again, this was all new to me because I felt I was OK with what was happening. It happened at the same time that I was contemplating divorce so my heart was really on overdrive.

I was torn between – 'let it all crumble, let things fall apart and have a nervous breakdown' or 'fight for my sanity, my dignity and work through what was happening with my head held high'. I remember hearing the words 'I can't do this anymore', 'I can't take this anymore', 'I can't cope' 'I should give up and give out'. The more I dwelt on those words and took them to be my own thoughts, the more panic I felt.

I had to accept, certain situations were beyond me, and no matter how good my intentions were about a given situation, it just will not turn out the way I want it. I had to accept, things need to fall apart sometimes but it does not mean, I have to also fall apart. When things fall apart they can be pieced back together with time, but there is a great risk of no return if I let myself fall apart. So, I decided to flee from certain situations but fight for my sanity and mindfulness. I bless the day I found God. He alone can take credit for helping me through it.

I pray for you today as you read this, just as God saw me through, and still is seeing me through, He will do same for you. You will testify one day that it all worked out. The situation may not have worked out as planned, but God will work out a better plan for you.

Misery's Comfort

Misery likes company for comfort. All of a sudden the failure seemed as if it wasn't my fault since other people also failed. I would then diminish the intelligence of those who passed by saying, they had help or they were not as busy as I was so they had enough time to study. However secretly I wished I was not part of the losers and rather part of those who passed.

It is comforting to be amongst those with the same adverse situation. It's a coping mechanism but a very dangerous one. It helps for a little while but to be a victor rather than a victim, you need to recognise if this is the best way to cope with things and decide to overcome them. It is very crippling and can lead to further failures in life. Then the cycle continues.

When you are a victim in a bad situation, to feel comforted you may find some consolation knowing others are also unhappy. In fact, you may be so busy drawing comfort from other people's misery, you forget you have to be victorious for your own self.

Never base your wellbeing on the downfall of your enemies. As the Bible warns:

> "Do not rejoice when your enemy falls, and do not let your heart be glad when he stumbles; lest the Lord see it, and it displease Him, and He turn away His wrath from him."

(Proverbs 24:17-18)

Yes, it will give you 'closure' when justice is served, but in order to overcome being labelled a victim for the rest of your life, you have to take control back from that situation and decide not to depend on justice happening before you live your life as a victor.

Writing this I realise how important it was for me to understand this concept. It was absolutely crucial for my sanity, my healing and my victory to not rely on bad things happening to those who betrayed me in order to feel 'closure' or in order for me to move on with my life.

It still is the most painful 'growing up' I have had to do. Jesus says we should pray for our offenders:

> "But I say to you, love your enemies, bless those who curse you, do good to those who hate you, and pray for those who spitefully use you and persecute that you may be sons of your Father in heaven; for He makes His sun rise on the evil and on the good, and sends rain on the just and on the unjust. For if you love those who love you, what reward have you? Do not even the tax collectors do the same? Therefore, you shall be perfect, just as your Father in heaven is perfect."
>
> *(Matthew 5:44-48)*

Notice how 'perfection is almost going against 'natural feelings'. God is asking us to do the opposite of what we 'feel' like doing to our enemies as part of being perfected to be like Him!

How could I keep praying for my enemies when they had caused me much pain? Oh, but Jesus, sweet Jesus, helped me to do it. He enabled me to not seek out for bad news about those who had done me wrong in order to feel better. It is one of the hardest things to do.

How? Everyone goes through bad times and good times. I took comfort rather in knowing, everyone goes through ups and downs. Hence, there was no point taking comfort in people's misery because others would also take comfort in mine when the time comes. There was no point waiting to draw comfort from people's bad times because their bad times may not come on cue when you want it to!

What an emotional roller-coaster many of us put ourselves through! No wonder some forever talk about that one time someone hurt them or they never seem to get over the rape or the evil done to them. Please do not get me wrong, by all means find what works for you but understand, you cannot base your happiness on the sorrow of others. You will forever remain a victim of your own making. Rather find those who survived, those who overcame, those who are doing well despite their situation and take comfort in their progress knowing and being hopeful, the same God who helped them through it, will also help you through it.

Accept, it is indeed painful to see the wicked flourish, King David also lamented about this:

> "For I was envious of the boastful, when I saw the prosperity of the wicked. For there are no pangs in their death, but their strength is firm. They are not in trouble as other men, nor are they plagued like other men ... when I thought how to understand this, it was too painful for me until I went into the sanctuary of God; Then I understood their end."
>
> *(Psalm 73:3-5, 16-17)*

Take back control, surround yourself with people who want you to be better than those who simply provide fleeting comfort by encouraging your misery.

Get over yourself

There is nothing more pathetic-looking than a pity party for two. That is – you and the chimp on the shoulder recounting how the world is having fun without you.

One of the things that helped me get over some of life's challenges, is to get over myself. You are well on your way to becoming a victorious person if you can just speak the truth to yourself. It is cowardice to blame everyone for your state and not be able to frankly analyse your role in the situation. Although there are certain things that happened which were not your fault, you still play a role in how you let it affect you. That makes you a participant in the events.

It was one of the hardest things I had to do but it needed to be done. I had to understand and accept my part in the state of my marriage. Even though it was no excuse what he did to me and no matter my failings, no one should be subjected to such humiliation and I certainly did not beg for it. But, it's a big 'but' I had to accept, some of my actions or lack thereof would have been misconstrued and therefore used as a contributory factor to my partner's infidelity.

After throwing a pity party or two for myself and others in attendance specifically self-condemnation, bitterness, shame and rejection, I decided the party was no fun at all, so it was short lived. I'm not and will not be the first person that's had the rough childhood, been fatherless, been rejected, been cheated on, been laid off work and other undesirable misfortunes. I am not less of a human because of what I have been through. It does not matter if people do not subscribe to my line of thinking or if some people chose not to like me. 'C'est la vie! que sera sera!'

The truth is, it is not everyone I necessarily like but I 'love' them as Christ commands us; therefore, not everyone should be expected to like me or agree with me. It is not everyone I particularly agree with and though I am loved by God, I am not exempted from life's hard knocks. I have to go through hard choices like everyone else.

Understand this, you cannot keep playing the victim due to everything that happens to you. Get over it. Please forgive me if I sound brash but sometimes truth hurts but it is liberating. Many people constantly throw a pity party for themselves at every sign of a differing opinion or opposition. This is exhibited in phrases such as 'Maybe they don't like me', 'they are racist', 'they like this person more than me', 'I am not loved'. Though I admit, some of these thoughts and sayings may have traces of truth in them, it is not enough to keep running away from challenges or waiving the 'I am a victim' banner all the time.

The truth is, the world celebrates victim-hood. Many people have found a 'new' identity in their state of being a victim of something. They bask in pity from people, and raise funds from people's pity. The society we live in is conditioning us to respond to sad stories in a selfish way. People will 'show acts of kindness' not necessarily because it's a sad situation and they genuinely want to help, but because they want to be 'seen doing good' and they feel less humane if they don't. As a result, a lot of fraudulent 'cry for help' situations have arisen where people are now being emotionally manipulated to constantly give because of all the wrong that's happened to someone. God wants us to 'give cheerfully' not under emotional oppression! With all our best efforts we cannot eradicate poverty in the world.

Jesus said it Himself:

> "For you have the poor with you always,
> but Me you do not have always."
>
> *(Matthew 26:11)*

Do not subject yourself to just thinking about how bad things have been with you. Try and re-focus on how things could get better and that you have to grab life by the horns and use what you have to get what you want. This does not mean, you use a 'sorry' pity story to get ahead, but rather turn your messy story to a message of hope, turn your victimisation to steps to becoming victorious!

Tell yourself enough is enough with the self-pity because when all is said and done only those with a lion heart get the lion's share out of this life.

Victory in life is not a right, it's a fight

It's important to know who is backing you so you can overcome who and/or what is confronting you in life.

For me, the 'who' is God. Every day He finds a way to let me know I am His own even though sometimes I find it difficult to live up to my 'status'.

On my journey to becoming who I am today, my mind had a lot to ponder on. I heard a saying once: 'what is the use of the mind if cannot be changed'. I had built up a lot of 'bad thinking' habits or patterns, I later realised are contributory to daily defeats.

Here are a few keys on how to fight for daily victories:

- Understand your reward in life is determined by the kind of problem you are prepared to solve for others. You will find fulfilment and victory when you fulfil the need of others.
- Pay attention to what takes your attention. Anything that takes your attention controls you. What controls you can destroy you. Its takes strength and honesty to catch yourself being distracted and admit its impact on you.
- Look out for guidance and instructions. It's important to know when guidance is needed and to recognise instructions. It is within instructions we find our miracles. The Israelite's found their miracle in obeying instruction to go around the wall of Jericho seven times and make trumpet sounds. (see Joshua 6:1-27) Could it be, by obeying a simple instruction to clean out a room, you could find treasures you thought were once lost?
    - What a successful person will do daily, an unsuccessful person will do occasionally. Another key to your victory is in your daily routine. Decide to have little 'victories' each day by using your daily routine to build a successful lifestyle.
    - Do not compromise your tomorrow for today's pleasures. We must always look ahead to see what we need to do now to get there. Jesus fixed His eye on the Glory of His Father so much so

that the persecutions and trails He faced did not faze Him.

Don't force your way to have what is not yours. If you insist on taking something God did not give you, others will take what is yours. David forced himself on Uriah's Wife. God did not give her to him. That was the beginning of many more troubles for David. Many of us will frown on the thought of taking someone else's spouse, but we covet so much that we compromise on who we are in order to have what we covet, losing ourselves in the process. It's safer not to look for what God did not give you, but be content with what you have and who you are.

Call to Action

Think honestly about the time you have thrown a pity party for yourself.

Write down the things you feel have led you to become a victim. Then throw it away consciously, asking God to help you throw away the burden of being a victim as you throw away the paper.

Think about the people who seem to remind you of your ordeal, forcing you to recount the bad feelings without encouraging goods ones.

Then decide to let go. Go on. You can do it! Go and read:

- Matthew 9:1-8
- Matthew 18:23-35

"To err is human, to forgive is divine."[3]

Prayer

Father Lord, I pray for those reading this, I pray for Your grace for them to be strong and remain strong. I pray that the Love of God will embrace them and keep them under your wings forever. Amen

Endnotes

1: study.com/academy/lesson/general-adaptaonsyndrome-stages-definion-examples.html (accessed April 20, 2019).
2: verywellmind.com/what-is-the-fight-or-flight-response2795194 By Kendra Cherry Sept 21, 2018 reviewed by Steven Gans, MD (accessed April 20, 2019).
3: Topics, Sample Papers and Arcles Online for Free. (2016). "To err is Human, to forgive is Devine. [Online]" studymoose.com/to-err-is-human-to-forgive-is-devineessay (Accessed May 11, 2019).

Chapter 8

What Is In Your Hands?

By now you may have gathered, the main concept of this book is to encourage you to overcome rejection by using it to your advantage. Instead of it remaining a source of negativity, you can use it as an agent or catalyst for change in the right direction. In other words, use what you have or what you have been given to get what you want or where you want to be in life. To do this effectively, a lot of self-evaluation and analysis[1] has to take place. You have to take stock of what you have or what is in your hands, namely your talents, experiences, skills, imperfections and, most of all, the areas in your life you have control over. Once you identify or discover all these things, you will need to be determined to take advantage of your situation for a better outcome.

Remember, rejection is more than just an emotion; for most people it is a constant presence of ill will and failure. It is that overarching realisation you are not good enough for something, someone, or to fit in somewhere, and not quite deserving of good things happening to you. Therefore, it becomes necessary to do some soul searching and analysis of the areas where you have been rejected, work out what is true about you and what is not true, then begin to work on what is true to optimise it to your advantage.

As always, the best illustration I can use is myself. Sometime ago I experienced a major rejection at a place of work. It was a new career path for me, and though I had never been in that industry before, I really wanted to succeed and try my best. I gave it my best shot. I started noticing a few months into the job, some colleagues did not feel I was right for the job. I stuck out like a sore thumb. First of all, it was a male dominated role, predominately white and also with a lot of Asian males. Most were not particularly tolerant of my openness about my Christian faith either as I later found out. All these factors of course were not enough to make me cower or feel intimidated.

I worked harder, knowing I automatically had to prove myself and prove why I should remain in that position. Granted, this would not have been a problem of rejection as such if not for the fact, I noticed I was constantly being subjected to ad hoc 'ear pulling' for petty things I was either not involved in or of which I had been wrongly accused.

I was told in so many words, my face did not fit. Thankfully, I recognised when my time was up. I was caught between two hard choices 'stay and continue to prove myself despite the rejection I felt' or 'quit whilst I still could without risking an adverse release of contract. In the end both parties had to come to an agreement to part ways amicably. Technically, everyone was a winner. I was, of course, initially devastated my time with the company was up; it was a good company, which I genuinely liked and was loyal to it. But it was just not meant to be. The rejection I felt was real and profound because it was all happening at the same time – rejection in my marriage, in my church and now in my place of work. Once again, the questions began to torment me on the inside – Where do I fit? Where do I belong? What do I have that anyone wants or values? What am I supposed to be doing with my career? Why has this happened to me? I was out of work for two months. I cannot remember the last time I was out of work for that long.

However, I remember the Holy Spirit prompting me to use the situation to my advantage. He had provided for our upkeep, so I didn't need to worry about that. I decided to use that 'free' time to rebase myself. First of all, to rest, to spend some time with my daughter and to study. I discovered in the end God was helping me by being rejected at that time. You see, had I carried on in the role with the constant battle to prove myself, I may never catch up or match up. It would have taken a huge toll on my psyche, etc. It would have also meant a lot of compromise, which I'm not prepared to do. More importantly, I would not have met my new employer who have been nothing but a blessing to me at this time of my life.

I do not think my previous employers perhaps purposefully set out to reject me the way they did. They perhaps meant well, in that they made me realise the role was not for me.

God indeed had other plans, as He always does. God encouraged me to use the period of rejection as an agent of change, I used it to my advantage. Yes, my pride was wounded, and I still sometimes wonder 'what if' but I do not regret the experience it afforded me, and I don't regret my time there. It was all a learning curve for me and proved to me, I can do whatever I put my mind to do so long as God wants me to do it!

I started studying in a completely different field. Why not try something new, right? Yes, I did and I do enjoy it.

Dear Reader, I hope my experience will encourage you to always analyse why you think you have been rejected, honestly accept certain things are not meant to be and then look for ways to better yourself using any criticism you may have received. But whatever you do, avoid the temptation to crumble in the process, and do not let yourself dwell on the negatives.

Were you rejected from a certain sport because of your weight? Well, either get fit to feel great or join another sport that is indifferent to your weight. Were you rejected by someone because of your height, weight, traits? Accept, perhaps that person is not meant for you, and gravitate toward those who celebrate you not just tolerate you.

Are you facing rejection because you cannot sing as well as someone you know? Then perhaps you can write songs instead!

Below are a few examples of people across time in biblical history, past famous people and current celebrities who at some point in their lives experienced some major rejection, had a defection demotion, which was either used as a stepping stone to success or their failures and shortcomings were not enough to hinder their destiny.

Biblical Examples

Moses

He was a Law Giver, Prophet and universally recognised as the deliverer of his people, the Israelites, from slavery in Egypt. Biblical and human history also credit him with establishing Israel's judicial and religious systems.

Moses was the first abandoned child mentioned in the Bible, and the record of his stammer suggests he suffered with a speech defect. On the downside, he was a murderer, and married someone not approved by his people. Yet God used him to part the Red Sea and deliver his people from slavery.

A very interesting conversation between him and God illustrates precisely how God uses our shortcomings to promote us.

One day when he was tending his flock on Sinai, the mountain of God, the angel of the Lord appeared to him in a burning bush. After getting his attention in this way, God then engaged him in a conversation in which he commissioned him to deliver His people from cruel slavery at the hand of the Egyptians.

God wanted Moses to deliver a message to Pharaoh, the Egyptian king. The message from God was that he should let His people go for three days into the wilderness in order to make sacrifices to Him. Despite God re-assuring Moses, He would be with Him and enable him to do signs to convince pharaoh to let them go, Moses was reluctant to say yes to God's call.

Moses protested several times against being used by

God. First, he claimed to be inadequate to approach pharaoh and questioned his ability to lead the people of Israel out of Egypt. God patiently assured Moses of His Presence so he would not have to face Pharaoh alone.

Again, Moses protested, doubting whether the people would even know who God was, much less accept his message of salvation. Once more, God patiently listened, then re-assured Moses of His presence and was taught what to say to convince the people of Israel. God even told him His plans for Egypt and revealed His promise to redeem the people of Israel from oppression. But Moses was afraid of what people would say, feeling inadequate and focusing on his imperfection; he protested the third time. He was afraid people would not believe he was sent by God. (Exodus 3:1-22)

This time God continued by asking him what he had in his hand, to which he replied – "A shepherd staff." God proceeded to demonstrate three miraculous signs to Moses – turning the staff into a snake then back to a staff; his hand was withered by leprosy and then healed again. God assured him, if the first two signs did not convince the people, he should turn water into blood.

Even though God patiently answered and gave Moses signs and wonders to perform, Moses still did not feel confident enough to fulfil his calling.

> "… but Moses pleaded with the Lord, 'O Lord, I'm not very good with words. I never have been, and I'm not now, even though you have spoken to me. I get tongue-tied, and my words get tangled.'
> Then the Lord asked Moses, 'Who makes a person's mouth? Who decides whether people speak or do not

speak, hear or do not hear, see or do not see? Is it not I, the Lord? Now go! I will be with you as you speak, and I will instruct you in what to say.'

But Moses again pleaded, 'Lord, please! Send anyone else.' Then the Lord became angry with Moses. 'All right,' he said. 'What about your brother, Aaron the Levite? I know he speaks well, and look! He is on his way to meet you now. He will be delighted to see you. Talk to him, and put the words in his mouth. I will be with both of you as you speak, and I will instruct you both in what to do. Aaron will be your spokesman to the people. He will be your mouthpiece, and you will stand in the place of God for him, telling him what to say. And take your shepherd's staff with you, and use it to perform the miraculous signs I have shown you.'"

(Exodus 4:10-17)

From these very detailed conversations between God and Moses, we get a glimpse into how God the Father hears our prayers and send us a helper. Notice how He also patiently listens as we complain about our lacks and disadvantages in life. Therefore, if God can use a stutterer and a rod, then He can surely make something great of your life despite the limitations you possess.

King David

David was the second King of Israel, and from whose bloodline Jesus Christ was born. He is an important figure in Christianity, Judaism and Islam. Famous for slaying

Goliath the Giant, an enemy of Israel as a boy with a sling and stone.

David is arguably one of the most controversial characters in the Bible. He was rejected by his family. He murdered Uriah and took his widow to be his wife after sleeping with her when Uriah was still alive. He was a fugitive and an outlaw in his own country. At one point, his own son rebelled against him. David's life was in all kinds of mess.

Many of us can relate to David, either as the insignificant shepherd's boy, the troubled teenager, the fugitive youth, or the betrayed leader. We can all find ourselves in David's story.

The most read book in the Bible is arguably Psalms, mostly penned by David, all through his life. The Book of psalms is like a journal and hymnbook, which gives the reader insight into the love relationship the writer had with God, his struggles, doubts, low points, high points and his prayers.

Psalm 3 is a psalm of David, focusing on the time David fled from his son Absalom.

"O Lord, I have so many enemies; so many are against me. So many are saying, "God will never rescue him!"
Interlude
But you, O Lord, are a shield around me; you are my glory, the one who holds my head high.
I cried out to the Lord, and he answered me from his holy mountain. Interlude
I lay down and slept, yet I woke up in safety, for the Lord was watching over me I am not afraid of ten thousand enemies who surround me on every side.

> Arise, O Lord! Rescue me, my God! Slap all my enemies
> in the face shatter the teeth of the wicked
> Victory comes from you, O Lord. May you bless your
> people. Interlude."

(Psalm 3:1-8)

God still used David despite all his mistakes and more. He was still a friend of God. He was a great warrior and a God lover. His 'Journal' in many of the Psalms, is a blessing to many souls even to this day.

No matter how 'low' you find yourself, how insignificant you feel or what shortcomings you have, you are a masterpiece in God's hands to use for great things.

The boy with two fishes and five loaves

Though the boy's name is unknown, yet it was his lunch, which was used to miraculously feed thousands of people.

This story *(John 6:1-14)* is particularly inspiring because I am sure, like most of us, you would have thought nothing of it. The lunch would barely be enough for one person much less for thousands. But here is another classic example of how God can use the littlest, simplest of things to bring about a change in your life and that of others.

Jesus had finished talking to a huge crowd that followed him to the far side of the Sea of Galilee.

Being compassionate, He did not want to turn them away without feeding them so He asked Philip, one of the disciples, if he knew where to buy bread for them.

Phillip protested, they did not have enough money to feed such a crowd, but Jesus already had a plan.

Simon Peter's brother, Andrew, then pointed out a boy who had his lunch of five loaves and two fishes but doubted if that could be of any use.

But Jesus asked everyone to be seated and simply prayed over the five loaves of bread and two fishes, thanking God for what they had. Miraculously, not only did the boy's lunch feed more than five thousand people till they were full, but they had twelve baskets full of leftover! (John 6: 1-14)

Notice how Andrew evaluated what the boy brought. He had no faith or hope in what the boy had to offer. Many of us probably identify with the boy. What do I have compared to the plenty others have? There will be many people who sound like Andrew but thank God for Jesus – the One who never changes.

He is the same *"yesterday, today and forever"* (Hebrews 13:8).

If He could find great use for a little boy's lunch snack, then surely He has the power to turn the most insignificant thing in life to the most significant testimony of your life.

The woman with the Alabaster box

Here we learn of the story of a sinful woman who was forgiven because she used what she had to serve God.

Anyone who has ever done anything wrong will be inspired by the story of this unknown woman. Her most significant accomplishment in life came from using what she had on the most important person. Many have been rejected by religious sects and sadly by churches because they do not fit the category of 'holiness' or look as if they belong to the church.

The gifts, talents and services of people who do not fit into the 'religious' setting have been rejected and castigated just like this woman was rejected and labelled by the very people who 'followed' Jesus.

Yet, it is a great consolation, Jesus Himself did not reject her. He saw deeply into the motivation for her acts of love, worship and servanthood. He saw, she recognised she was wretched, sinful and unworthy yet she decided to use what she had and did what she could to serve Jesus.

One day Jesus was asked to dinner at the home of a Pharisee. Whilst they sat to eat, a woman who was considered to be a sinner by the Pharisees came kneeling at Jesus's feet to pour out an alabaster jar filled with expensive perfume.

She was moved to tears from the weight of her sin and shame that she began to weep, the tears fell on His feet so she wiped them off with her hair. She kissed his feet and kept pouring the perfume on them.

The Pharisee host judged her and felt Jesus should know better than allow a sinful woman to touch Him. Jesus, reading his thoughts told him of a story to teach us a very valuable lesson on forgiveness and acceptance:

"A man loaned money to two people – 500 pieces of silver to one and 50 pieces to the other. But neither of them could repay him, so he kindly forgave them both, cancelling their debts. Who do you suppose loved him more after that?' Simon answered, 'I suppose the one for whom he cancelled the larger debt.' 'That's right,' Jesus said. Then he turned to the woman and said to Simon, 'Look at this woman kneeling here. When I

entered your home, you didn't offer me water to wash
the dust from my feet, but she has washed them with
her tears and wiped them with her hair. You didn't Jesus
said. You didn't greet me with a kiss, but from the time
I first came in, she has not stopped kissing my feet. You
neglected the courtesy of olive oil to anoint my head,
but she has anointed my feet with rare perfume. I tell
you, her sins – and they are many – have been forgiven,
so she has shown me much love. But a person who is
forgiven little shows only little love.'

Then Jesus said to the woman, 'Your sins are forgiven.'
The men at the table said among themselves, 'Who is this
man, that he goes around forgiving sins?' And Jesus said
to the woman, 'Your faith has saved you; go in peace.'"

(Luke 7:41-50)

Dear reader, never ever let anyone or anything, including
your own insecurities, stop you from coming to Jesus just
as you are and with what you have to give in service to Him.

Jesus sees more deeply than any human can. Be
encouraged, to use everything you have for God including
your time, energy, money, background, colour, beauty, even
your hair! Use these to serve God who alone has the power
to forgive us for our sins!

Other Notable Examples

Albert Einstein

As a Physicist, he is famous for his theory of relativity and
the equation $E=mc^2$, which foreshadowed the development

of atomic power and the atomic bomb. Albert did not speak until he was four and did not read until he was seven. A few years later, he was expelled from school and was not admitted to the Zurich Polytechnic School. His elementary school teachers considered him lazy because he would ask abstract questions that made no sense to others. Albert had autism.

He persevered with his investigations, eventually formulating the theory of relativity – something that still does not make sense to most of us today!

Benjamin Franklin

A founding father of the United States of America, he was a writer, scientist, inventor, and a leading figure in the American struggle for independence. Franklin was the inventor of bifocal spectacles and the lightning rod – a material used to conduct electricity, used to protect a structure from a lightning strike. He helped draft the Declaration of Independence and the U.S. Constitution. However, He achieved all this despite being an elementary school dropout.

His family couldn't afford to finance his education after his 10th birthday, but that didn't stop him. He took every opportunity he could to learn so, he read books voraciously. Ironically, Franklin is now found in the history books that 10-year-old kids around the world read every day.

Thomas Edison

He was an inventor and business man. He is famous for inventing incandescent light bulb and one of the earliest motion picture cameras. He also created the world's first industrial research laboratory. He worked at Western Union where he used to secretly conduct experiments. Then, one night in 1867, he spilled some acid and it ate through the entire floor. He was fired and subsequently decided to just pursue inventing full time.

Edison may hold the record for the most failed attempts before reaching success on a single project. He failed several thousand times before inventing a functional light bulb. His response has become famous to entrepreneurs: *"I have not failed. I've just found 10,000 ways that won't work."*[1]

Walt Disney

He was an innovative animator and created the cartoon character Mickey Mouse. Disney began his career by being fired in 1919 by a newspaper, 'Kansas City Star', for not being creative enough. It is reported, his editor said he *"lacked imagination and had no good ideas."*

Later, his Mickey Mouse cartoons were rejected because they were deemed to be *"too scary for women."* If that wasn't enough, 'The Three Little Pigs' was also turned down because it only had four characters.

Interestingly we have the Disney Company today because Walt chose not to listen to any of his critics and press forward towards his dreams.

Oprah Winfrey

Best known for her talk show 'The Oprah Winfrey Show', which was the highest-rated television program of its kind in history. Oprah Winfrey's greatest accomplishments include being Chairwoman and CEO of both Harpo Productions and The Oprah Winfrey Network.

Oprah Winfrey was an evening news reporter and apparently was fired because she couldn't sever her emotions from her stories. Eventually she was fired as the producer of Baltimore's WJZ-TV. She was given a daytime TV show as a consolation and at last, she found her true calling. Since then, she has become a household name, and has won various awards and accolades for her work, including an Emmy Lifetime Achievement Award in 1998.

Michael Jordan

He was a professional Footballer from 1984-2003, and is arguably considered one of the best basketball players of all time.

As a kid, Jordan loved basketball and knew he wanted to make a career out of it, though no coach would give him a chance because he was 'short'. He was cut from his high school basketball team. After using an inside connection to get into a basketball camp from which players for college teams were chosen, Jordan got noticed by a coach – who still chose not to invite him to the team.

Jordan returned home discouraged but decided to prove the coach wrong. He once said, "I have missed over 9,000 shots in my career. I have lost almost 300 games. On 26 occasions I have been entrusted to take the game's winning shot, and I have missed. I have failed over and over and over again in my life. And that is why I succeed."[2] Jordan is now a member of the NBA Hall of Fame, and just about everyone would agree, he indeed succeeded. Jordan defied all of these things just to prove people wrong – he used the words of naysayers to jump through the hoops of failure to success.

Kris Carr

We all get hit by unforeseen obstacles. But for Carr, a wellness activist and cancer survivor, it was a rare cancer. Below is what she wrote about finding out she had cancer, [3] *"Why Me? – I felt like I was punched in the stomach by God,' she recalls. 'Cancer is such a frightening word. How could this be happening to me? Cancer happened to other people. I was young and vibrant. I was the Bud Girl, for Christ's sake. I felt like I was staring down the barrel of a gun, waiting to find out how many bullets were inside."*

There were 24 – to be exact – littering her liver and lungs.

Carr pressed the doctor on her options. *"Just try and live a normal life,"* he told her. With two dozen time bombs ticking inside her? *"How the hell could I do that? How could I live with cancer without thinking of dying every day?"* she wondered. Well, he offered, she could try to strengthen her immune system through diet and lifestyle changes.

He did not know it, but in that moment he planted the seeds for personal revolution, Carr says. *"I was not going to kick back and wait for the unknown. I was going to dive in and become a full-time healing junkie."*

Carr fought her disease head on with a new nutritional lifestyle, developing a career as a successful author and health coach in the process. Despite facing challenging circumstances from the start, she is now looked to as one the most knowledgeable experts on healthy living today.

Nick Vujicic

An Evangelist and Motivational speaker, Nick was born without arms or legs. He was born with an extremely rare congenital disorder known as 'phocomelia', which is characterised by the absence of legs and arms.

Nick struggled mentally, emotionally, and physically. Bullied at school, he attempted suicide when he was just 10 years old.

When you feel you have not been given equal opportunities in life to get ahead or to match up in life, what do you do? Should you sulk, complain, and be bitter? Why not? Perhaps we can learn a thing or two on how Nick overcame what he does not have, and used what he had to achieve great things.

Eventually coming to terms with his disability, Nick decided to become vocal about living with disabilities and finding hope and meaning in life. Below is a glimpse of the things he has achieved despite his circumstances:

- When Nick proposed to his wife in 2011, he used his mouth to put the ring on her finger.
- Despite the lack of limbs, he went on to father their four children, two sons and twin daughters.
- He can write, type 45 words per minute, swim, answer the phone and kick tennis balls extremely far.
- He started his first business, Life without Limbs, a non-profit organisation when he was only 17.

- Nick graduated with a Bachelor of Commerce at the age of 21 from Griffith University. He had a double major of financial planning and accountancy.

Nick hasn't let the fact of having no arms and no legs stop him from achieving his dreams. He is a devout Christian, believing, God loves everyone equally, and has taken it upon himself to spread this message to everyone around the world. His life story has inspired millions of people all over the world. And it should also inspire you and me!

Nick often says he keeps a pair of shoes in his closet, because he believes in miracles! [4] Here are a few of his inspirational quotes:

> "If God can use a man without arms and legs to be His hands and feet, then He will certainly use any willing heart!"

> "I have the choice to be angry with God for what I don't have, or be thankful for what I do have."

And my personal favourite:

> "God can heal you without changing your circumstance."

Nick's story particularly resonates with me because, on the face of it, to an untrained heart it would seem, God wanted to make him or others like him to suffer. It would seem everyone else could be rejected due to the fault of their actions, but for people like Nick they were not given any choice. They were born with such a disadvantage compared to others. But with a transformed heart and the viewpoint of regarding God as a loving God, all I see is God's mercy and miraculous wonders in Nick's life.

No, God is not unfair or unjust. Time and chance happen to everyone, we are just given different tools of life to work with. How you use it is up to you. Ultimately, you're no different to the people aforementioned. We will all fail at one point or another. The important thing is to learn how to overcome failure and rejection, and to keep pushing forward towards your dreams.

Whilst I do not necessary ascribe to all the philosophies of those listed above, I do believe they are extraordinary examples for us to see, we must be determined to use what we have to get to where we are destined to be. The journey between your current status and your destiny is filled with unexpected twists and turns but ultimately it is yours for the taking.

Prayer Time

- Lord, help me to recognise and appreciate that there is a reason I do not have certain things which others take for granted.
- Teach me to use what I do have to better myself and those around me.
- Thank you for yesterday, today and for your re-assurance that my tomorrow is in Your hands.

Endnotes

1: BrainyQuote, "Thomas A. Edison Quotes" www.brainyquote. com/quotes/ thomas_a_edison_132683 (accessed April 27, 2019).

2: BrainyQuote, "Michael Jordan Quotes" www.brainyquote. com/quotes/ michael_jordan_167379 (accessed April 27, 2019).

3: Lisa Stein, "Living with Cancer: Kris Carr's Story" hps:/ / www.scienficamerican.com/arcle/living-withcancer-kris-carr/ (Accessed April, 27 2019).

4: Movaon – Inspiraon "Nick Vujicic, a man with no limbs who teaches people how to get up" movaoninspiraon. weebly. com/nick-vujicic.html (Accessed April, 27 2019).

Chapter 9

God of the Hills
and Valleys

Many people have struggled with the existence of God because they cannot understand why a good God can allow terrible experiences to happen to people. Frankly, I have thought so myself. Through all of life's dealings I have of course questioned God over a lot of things which happened to me whether good or bad. You see it is perfectly normal to ask God, *"Why?"* The only challenge is, if you are bold enough to question God, then you must be prepared for His response – whatever it is.

There are a few people in biblical times who have been bold enough to question God, or to express doubt in God's promises. I hope as we read through their experiences, we can receive answers to our own questions, drive away doubts and calm fears. The highest achieving human at his best is still a human. We see in part, and we are limited

– limited in resources, time and space. Even with all the witty inventions, ground-breaking technology and mind-blowing discoveries, we are still playing catch-up to an all-knowing God. In fact, the more things we discover, the more questions we have about the universe and ourselves.

> "Now we see things imperfectly, like puzzling reflections in a mirror, but then we will see everything with perfect clarity. All that I know now is partial and incomplete, but then I will know everything completely, just as God now knows me completely."
>
> *(1 Corinthians 13:12, NLT)*

Despite our human limitations, we have been able to achieve some truly amazing things. Our intelligence can only grow and the human race is a very powerful force. The power of the human mind and the will of the human spirit cannot be taken lightly. It is said, angels in heaven discover more of God through His dealings with the human race. We are so complex yet predictable, so strong yet so weak. It is amazing to be human – in fact, so amazing, many have become deceived into thinking they are gods, can overthrow/dethrone God, or they are more powerful than God. Some even boldly yet foolishly say, 'There is no God.'

> *"Only fools say in their hearts, 'There is no God.'"*
>
> *(Psalm 14:1 NLT)*

A grave mistake to make is to think, God is only good when things are good, when things are on the high, when on the hilltop. God still remains a good God when things are low, when things are not as expected and down in the valleys. God is so sovereign, He does not feel threatened by our lack of faith neither is He provoked to anger by our lack of patience. He is very comfortable in letting us ask questions or express our unhappiness about how things are going. Just try not to attack His character or blaspheme against His Holy Spirit whilst you're at it. He makes it clear that His abilities exceed ours:

> "My thoughts are nothing like your thoughts,' says the Lord.' … and my ways are far beyond anything you could imagine. For just as the heavens are higher than the earth, so my ways are higher than your ways and my thoughts higher than your thoughts.'"
>
> *(Isaiah 55:8-9, NLT)*

So, is it wrong to question God?

We can get the answer in the Bible where we see people like Habakkuk questioning God. Habakkuk, Jeremiah and David asked God the same question many of us are still asking today.

In the following conversation with God, we see Jeremiah questioned why he was chosen:

> "I knew you before I formed you in your mother's womb. Before you were born I set you apart and appointed you as my prophet to the nations.'
> 'O Sovereign Lord,' I said, 'I can't speak for you! I'm too young!' The Lord replied, 'Don't say, – I'm too young – for you must go wherever I send you and say

> whatever I tell you, and don't be afraid of the people, for
> I will be with you and will protect you. I, the Lord, have
> spoken!'"
>
> *(Jeremiah 1:5-8)*

David asked God why evil seemed to win and the reason for His silence:

David questioned why people got away with not accepting God and not helping the poor or their fellow human beings because of their pride. It appeared, wicked people were instead prospering and going unpunished. They threatened and carried out evil against the innocent, yet they thought God's hands were tied because nothing bad ever seemed to happen to them. He pleaded with God to punish them for all their wickedness, and answer the cries of their victims seeking justice and comfort.

> "The wicked are too proud to seek God. They seem to
> think that God is dead. Yet they succeed in everything
> they do. They do not see your punishment awaiting
> them. They sneer at all their enemies. They think,
> 'Nothing bad will ever happen to us! We will be free of
> trouble forever!'"
>
> *(Psalm 10:4-6, NLT)*

Have you ever harboured or expressed doubts about your faith? At some point in life, almost everyone has asked nagging questions about their faith – doubts about God, the Bible, or key elements of Christianity.

It is unhelpful to doubt God and His promises for us.

"If any of you lacks wisdom, you should ask God, who
gives generously to all without finding fault, and it will
be given to you. But when you ask, you must believe
and not doubt, because the one who doubts is like a
wave of the sea, blown and tossed by the wind.
That person should not expect to receive anything from
the Lord. Such a person is double-minded and unstable
in all they do."

(James 1:5-8 NIV)

However, doubt is part of the human condition. The Bible
contains many profiles of people who doubted – some of
them great heroes of faith!

Below are more Bible heroes who experienced doubt.
Take note of God's response to doubt as you read each
account.

Sarah and Abraham doubted God's Promise

Abraham is known as the 'father of faith'; however, before
assuming this position he and his wife Sarah went through
a very trying time in their walk with God. Throughout their
lifetime of challenges and trials both followed God faithfully.
God made a promise to them, they would give birth to a
son in their old age – Abraham was a hundred years old
and Sarah was 90 years of age. They could not quite bring
themselves to believe it. In fact, they both laughed at the
prospect. Such was the extent of their doubt, Sarah devised
a way for them to have a child independently of God – she
persuaded Abraham to sleep with her Handmaiden, Hagar,

and Ishmael was the result. But as far as God was concerned, he was not the 'Son of Promise' who was still to be born to them by supernatural means.

> "Then God said, 'Yes, but your wife Sarah will bear you a son, and you will call him Isaac. I will establish my covenant with him as an everlasting covenant for his descendants after him. And as for Ishmael, I have heard you: I will surely bless him; I will make him fruitful and will greatly increase his numbers. He will be the father of twelve rulers, and I will make him into a great nation. But my covenant I will establish with Isaac, whom Sarah will bear to you by this time next year.' When he had finished speaking with Abraham, God went up from him."
>
> *(Genesis 17:19-22)*

Reading this passage helps us to relate it to our own insecurities and doubts. God is not opposed to us stumbling in our faith as it is expected. We must only be careful not to have a prolonged or permanent loss of faith. We should build our faith on the things God has done in the past, and on His Word. There is nothing too hard for God. Once their son Isaac was born, Abraham's trust in God had grown so great, he was willing even to sacrifice him for God when asked. Hence, he became an example of a man who showed tremendous faith and total trust in God. Such will be said of you and me, by God's grace and in Jesus Name, Amen.

Gideon tests God

Gideon was chosen by God for a special purpose, but he doubted his calling and tested God twice, challenging God to provide proof of His reliability through a series of miracles, before he would believe he was called. God indeed has a wonderful sense of humour, so He indulged Gideon.

"So, he said to Him, 'O my Lord, how can I save Israel? Indeed, my clan is the weakest in Manasseh, and I am the least in my father's house.'

So, Gideon said to God, 'If You will save Israel by my hand as You have said look, I shall put a fleece of wool on the threshing floor; if there is dew on the fleece only, and it is dry on all the ground, then I shall know that You will save Israel by my hand, as You have said.' And it was so. When he rose early the next morning and squeezed the fleece together, he wrung the dew out of the fleece, a bowlful of water.

Then Gideon said to God, 'Do not be angry with me, but let me speak just once more: Let me test, I pray, just once more with the fleece; let it now be dry only on the fleece, but on all the ground let there be dew.'

And God did so that night. It was dry on the fleece only, but there was dew on all the ground.

(Judges 6:15, 36-40, NIV)

In the end through Gideon, God led the Israelites to victory. God used him to turn the tide against Israel's oppressors. Perhaps, like Gideon many of us know God is doing wonders, but just don't think it will be through '*us*'.

Thomas Doubts the Resurrection

Most of us have heard of 'doubting Thomas'. I would like to think, in heaven Thomas will find this story somewhat amusing every time it is read! Is it possible, someone so close to Jesus, someone who had perhaps spent *years* witnessing miracles, travelling with Christ, and learning at Jesus' feet as one of Jesus' own disciples could ever doubt, his master had been raised from the dead? Well Thomas did. There is so much to learn from Thomas's experience. Notably, eight days went by before he saw Jesus. He had been away from the other disciples, so he must have had a lot of time for questions and for doubt to plague his mind.

"One of the twelve disciples, Thomas (nicknamed the Twin), was not with the others when Jesus came. They told him, 'We have seen the Lord!'
But he replied, 'I won't believe it unless I see the nail wounds in his hands, put my fingers into them, and place my hand into the wound in his side.'
Eight days later the disciples were together again, and this time Thomas was with them. The doors were locked; but suddenly, as before, Jesus was standing among them. 'Peace be with you,' he said. Then he said to Thomas, 'Put your finger here, and look at my hands. Put your hand into the wound in my side. Don't be faithless any longer. Believe!' 'My Lord and my God!' Thomas exclaimed. Then Jesus told him, 'You believe because you have seen me. Blessed are those who believe without seeing me.'"

(John 20:24-29, NLT)

Notice in each case, God's response to request for proof (genuine doubt) is not wrath but patience; far from punishing His doubting followers, God honours those who seek after Him with earnest questions. Let us proclaim the sentiments in Mark 9:15 – "*I believe; help my unbelief!*" Far from bringing about judgement and despair, those experiences of doubt usually lead to a deeper faith.

Apart from doubt, there are times when we may want to question God regarding a matter. As mentioned above, Habakkuk asked God:

"*Why is this evil happening?*" God later indulged him with an answer which made him rejoice in the Lord. The difference between Habakkuk and most people still searching for the answer is, his question was coming from a sincere heart. Habakkuk's First Complaint:

'How long, O Lord, must I call for help?

But you do not listen!

Violence is everywhere!" I cry, but you do not come to save.

Must I forever see these evil deeds?

Why must I watch all this misery?

Wherever I look,

I see destruction and violence. I am surrounded by people who love to argue and fight.

The law has become paralysed, and there is no justice in the courts.

The wicked far outnumber the righteous, so that justice has become perverted.' The Lord replied,

'Look around at the nations; look and be amazed!

For I am doing something in your own day,

something you wouldn't believe even if someone told you about it.

I am raising up the Babylonians, a cruel and violent people.

They will march across the world and conquer other lands.
They are notorious for their cruelty and do whatever they like.
Their horses are swifter than cheetahs
and fiercer than wolves at dusk.
Their charioteers charge from far away.
Like eagles, they swoop down to devour their prey.
On they come, all bent on violence.
Their hordes advance like a desert wind, sweeping captives
ahead of them like sand.
They scoff at kings and princes and scorn all their fortresses.
They simply pile ramps of earth against their
walls and capture them!
They sweep past like the wind and are gone.
But they are deeply guilty, for their own strength is their god.

Habakkuk's Second Complaint

O Lord my God, my Holy One, you who are eternal surely you
do not plan to wipe us out?
Lord, our Rock, you have sent these Babylonians to correct us, to
punish us for our many sins.
But you are pure and cannot stand the sight of evil.
Will you wink at their treachery?
Should you be silent while the wicked swallow up people more
righteous than they?
Are we only fish to be caught and killed?
Are we only sea creatures that have no leader?
Must we be strung up on their hooks and caught in their nets
while they rejoice and celebrate?
Then they will worship their nets and
burn incense in front of them.

"These nets are the gods who have
made us rich!" they will claim.
Will you let them get away with this forever?
Will they succeed forever in their heartless conquests?
I will climb up to my watchtower and stand at my guard post.
There I will wait to see what the Lord says and how he will
answer my complaint.' Then the Lord said to me,
'Write My answer plainly on tablets, so that a runner can carry
the correct message to others.
This vision is for a future time.
It describes the end, and it will be fulfilled.
If it seems slow in coming, wait patiently,
for it will surely take place.
It will not be delayed ...

God then goes on to address the wicked, the proud who think they can get away with evil with no judgement in sight.

"What good is an idol carved by man, or a cast image
that deceives you? How foolish to trust in your own
creation – a god that can't even talk! What sorrow
awaits you who say to wooden idols, 'Wake up and save
us! To speechless stone images you say, 'Rise up and
teach us!' Can an idol tell you what to do? They may be
overlaid with gold and silver, but they are lifeless inside.
But the Lord is in his holy Temple. Let all the earth be
silent before him."

Habakkuk was struggling to understand God's approach in dealing with the wicked, especially seeing how much God's chosen people were suffering in the hands of evil people. He complained to God and made his own thoughts known about what was happening to his people.

From God's responses, Habakkuk could see, God is not slow to act against the wicked, neither is God short-sighted that He cannot see how evil the world is. Ultimately from where God sits, He sees it all and knows exactly what to do. He will indeed make all things right in the right time – His time. We just have to trust Him, even when it looks like evil is reigning.

With this understanding, Habakkuk writes:

> I have heard all about you, Lord. I am filled
> with awe by your amazing works.
> In this time of our deep need, help us again
> as you did in years gone by.
> And in your anger, remember your mercy.
> Even though the fig trees have no blossoms, and there
> are no grapes on the vines; even though the olive crop
> fails, and the fields lie empty and barren;
> even though the flocks die in the fields, and the cattle
> barns are empty, yet I will rejoice in the Lord!
> I will be joyful in the God of my salvation!
> The Sovereign Lord is my strength!
> He makes me as surefooted as a deer,
> able to tread upon the heights."
>
> *(Habakkuk Chapters 1-3 selected verses)*

Dear reader, as we see from the conversation between God and Habakkuk, we really do have a patient and loving God. He does not delight in making us suffer neither does He take pleasure in our pain. He wants to help us and protect us, but we must also remember to do our part:

> "Listen! the Lord's arm is not too weak to save you, nor is His ear too deaf to hear you call. It's your sins that have cut you off from God, because of your sins, He has turned away and will not listen anymore."
>
> *(Isaiah 59:1-2)*

Sin is a major blockage in receiving answers to our questions and solutions to our problems. It skews our judgement and perceptions of things. Sins automatically makes it difficult for us to boldly approach God with our cares and legitimate questions. Do I have to be perfect before I can speak or challenge a perfect God? No, but you can only boldly do it and expect a change if you have a right standing with Him.

I have heard people say on many occasions during evangelism or just general faith talk, they have stopped believing in God because He did not answer a prayer to cure a dying grandma or some other genuine request.

I can honestly say, not all of my prayers have been answered. Ultimately, we see in part, and there are many reasons why some of our prayers are not answered.

However, for some who say they lost faith in God because of an unanswered prayer, I say this: I know fully well, by Gods' standard of holiness, I have fallen short. Therefore, any 'blessing' or 'promise' of an answered prayer from God is indeed not a 'right' but a 'privilege'.

It is important to first have this understanding and accept, though God hears every prayer regardless of our sins, He does not have to respond to every request. It is unreasonable to expect God to 'jump' when you ask Him to do something.

So, if you have stopped believing in Him because of a yet unanswered prayer, then I can only pray, God will heal your heart.

However, to constantly taint His Holy Character because He has not granted something is very self-centred of us. God declares:

> "… I will be gracious to whom I will be gracious,
> and I will have compassion on whom I will have
> compassion."
>
> *(Exodus 33:19)*

Even the most well-meaning human being does not respond to 'every request' no matter how genuine. How much more does this apply to God who knows the thoughts and intentions of man. He knows our deepest, darkest acts of rebellion and disobedience. He sees our selfish motives and has to balance our selfish interest with that of others.

A farmer prays for rain, a traveller prays for clear and dry skies. Who should God listen to? Indeed, it must be tough being God!

The problem is, many people often question God with a rebellious and untrusting heart. Not really trying to get an answer but to attack His character because God allowed or did not allow something to happen. This in itself amounts to sin because it is prideful. The Prophet Isaiah throws some light on this when he considers the actions and attitudes of God's people.

God is all powerful and mighty. He has power to intervene in our situation and help us. He has the power to deliver us from evil; however, He does not intervene in our affairs because we have not invited Him into our lives, or our sins have become a stumbling block. Sin separates us from God's love. Innocent blood is shed all the time, there is so much injustice in the world, there is deceit and wickedness everywhere and there is no regard or reverence for God. As a result, the prayers of many are not being heard, and He will repay them according to what they have done.

Sin, Confession and Redemption

"For our offenses are many in your sight,
and our sins testify against us.
Our offenses are ever with us, and we acknowledge our
iniquities: rebellion and treachery against the Lord,
turning our backs on our God, inciting revolt and
oppression, uttering lies our hearts have conceived.
So, justice is driven back, and righteousness stands at
a distance; truth has stumbled in the streets, honesty
cannot enter. Truth is nowhere to be found, and
whoever shuns evil becomes a prey.
The Lord looked and was displeased that there was no
justice. He saw that there was no one, He was appalled
that there was no one to intervene; so, His own arm
achieved salvation for Him, and His own righteousness
sustained him.
He put on righteousness as his breastplate, and the
helmet of salvation on his head; he put on the garments

of vengeance and wrapped himself in zeal as in a cloak.

According to what they have done, so will he repay

wrath to his enemies and retribution to His foes; He will

repay the islands their due."

(Isaiah 59:12-18, NLT)

Wisdom problem

Most of the time our problems can be solved simply by applying wisdom to the situation. Instead of just blaming God for poverty and lack in your life, why not check your spending habits, high interest loans and debts, lack of frugality and so forth, and apply wisdom to your situation. Therefore, overcome poverty through wisdom.

Instead of questioning the existence of God after a divorce, why not look inward to see if your actions were contributory to the situation. Could it be, by applying wisdom, not just worldly wisdom but first and foremost Godly wisdom, we would have avoided the rejection or been able to handle it better.

Instead of blaming God for lack of peace in the world or even blaming the devil for every mistake you make, why not apply wisdom in every day decisions so the world can be a better place as better choices are made.

It is one thing to ask God why and another thing to doubt His goodness and His existence. In confusing situations and in matters beyond your control, pray for wisdom and expect an answer.

"If you need wisdom, ask our generous God, and he will give it to you. He will not rebuke you for asking.

But when you ask him, be sure that your faith is in God
alone. Do not waver, for a person with divided loyalty
is as unsettled as a wave of the sea that is blown and
tossed by the wind."

(James 1:5-6)

Even as believing Christians, though we are sinful by nature
but no longer deemed 'sinners'. We still doubt and question
God when things are not going well. Although this is
normal, we must always remember that we do not see into
the future to know how it will work out, or to see just how
God is working things out for us. Sometimes we might say,
"why me God?" and later find out, the answer is, "if not
you, then who?" And there is always a bonus. For example,
if the rejection did not happen at work you would not have
started the most amazing career or be self-employed.

Always thank God for being alive to experience 'life',
even though you might not know what to do and how to
overcome the pain you feel. Leave everything to Him, trust
with all your heart that God knows precisely what He is
doing, in His time He will make all things beautiful again.
It is best to accept, all our questioning does not move God
to action, only faith can move Him. Neither is He subject to
human scrutiny or judgement because He is infallible.

"Don't worry about anything; instead, pray about
everything. Tell God what you need and thank him for all
he has done. Then you will experience God's peace, which
exceeds anything we can understand. His peace will guard
your hearts and minds as you live in Christ Jesus."

(Philippians 4:6-7)

"… for who can know the Lord's thoughts? Who knows
enough to teach him?' But we understand these things,
for we have the mind of Christ."

(1 Corinthians 2:16, NLT)

"Who is able to advise the Spirit of the Lord? Who
knows enough to give him advice or teach him?"

(Isaiah 40:13)

Sometimes the questions we ask raise more doubt and fear than faith and substance even when we ask legitimate questions. This is because we are asking from our point of view and forget, we are limited in what we see and limited in our understand of the universe. So, when we question an infallible God with a fallible mind, we get an 'incomplete picture'. This is perhaps why faith impresses God.

"… and it is impossible to please God without faith.
Anyone who wants to come to him must believe that
God exists and that H rewards those who sincerely
seek Him."

(Hebrews 11:6 NLT)

In other words, when it seems as if God is not doing anything, He is doing everything you and I cannot do or see. He is working behind the scenes.

"… I am certain that God, who began the good work
within you, will continue his work until it is finally
finished on the day when Christ Jesus returns."

(Philippians 1:6)

"This is what the Lord says: 'You will be in Babylon for seventy years, but then I will come and do for you all the good things I have promised, and I will bring you home again. For I know the plans I have for you,' says the Lord 'They are plans for good and not for disaster, to give you a future and a hope.'"

(Jeremiah 29:10-11)

"And we know that God causes everything to work together[a] for the good of those who love God and are called according to his purpose for them."

(Romans 8:28)

We can take comfort from God's Word, which reminds us, we cannot have answers to all our questions in life. We see in part, and perhaps it is for a reason, we do not know all the answers to life's many questions. Could we really handle the truth about everything?

"Now our knowledge is partial and incomplete, and even the gift of prophecy reveals only part of the whole picture! But when the time of perfection comes, these partial things will become useless.
When I was a child, I spoke and thought and reasoned as a child. But when I grew up, I put away childish things. Now we see things imperfectly, like puzzling reflections in a mirror, but then we will see everything with perfect clarity. All that I know now is partial and incomplete, but then I will know everything completely, just as God now knows me completely."

(1 Corinthians 13:9-12)

If God were to answer every question, we may not be able to handle it. If God were to show us every spiritual activity or show us all the demons and angels as they operate, we may become fearful. If God were to show us all the evil thoughts and plans of people against us or our loved ones, we might become paranoid. If God were to really answer every question you have ever asked in your heart, would you be able to process it, without having even more questions? It does not mean we should not ask but we should rather ask in reverence to God.

Accept, there are and will always be certain things beyond our control and that indeed God knows best. Let Him be God.

Say this Prayer:

Lord, I pray you grant me the grace and strength to accept the things I cannot change.

Give me wisdom in all I do and help me each day to overcome temptation to fear and doubt your plans for me.

Thank you, Lord, for all you do for me that I see and do not see.

May I trust in you more and more each day. In Jesus Name, Amen.

Chapter 10

You Are What You Say

"Death and life are in the power of the tongue, and
those who love it will eat its fruit."

(Proverbs 18:21)

Words can be used as a defence as well as a weapon.
You cannot outlive your own words and you can
shape your destiny by what you say. God created the
universe through words, He breathed life into lifeless clay
and it became the first man whom He called Adam.

"For when He spoke, the world began!
It appeared at His command."

(Psalm 33:9)

We are like God in our creative abilities so therefore, we
also have the ability to use our words to create 'our world'. In
speech therapy, I was taught the way our words are formed

is also connected to how we breathe, i.e., in connection to the diaphragm. Therefore, when we speak about something we also 'breathe life' into it, just as God breathed life into us. There are various self-help books including some on nutrition and substance abuse in terms of what we take into our bodies. Notice how it hurts sometimes when you hear some negative feedback about yourself from either someone relatively unknown or people you know. Depending on the kind of words spoken over your life, it is still possible to overcome them because they are spoken by others. The saddest part is when the person who speaks the worst things about you is You. The mouth is not very far from the ears so whatever you say to yourself, will have the greatest effect.

It is important to understand, in order to use rejection as an agent of success, we have to learn to speak positively and confidently over our own lives. This world is a cruel place, and many harsh words will be spoken to discourage you, whether purposefully or otherwise. Therefore, it is up to you to encourage yourself, and learn to be self-motivating.

Notice how David encouraged himself in the Lord:

> "Now David was greatly distressed, for the people spoke of stoning him, because the soul of all the people was grieved, every man for his sons and his daughters. But David strengthened himself in the Lord his God."
>
> *(1 Samuel 30:6)*

On many occasions when feeling low, he would speak to his own soul:

"... why are you cast down, O my soul? And why are
you disquieted within me? Hope in God, for I shall yet
praise Him for the help of His countenance."

(Psalm 42:5)

I have met a lot of people who echo the words of their critics.
Listen, people may tell you what you are doing wrong, learn
from it and move on. Do not become your own enemy by
constantly regurgitating the opinion of others, especially if
it was not coming from a good place.

Growing up I heard a lot of negative things – 'Your
hands are destructive', 'everything you touch breaks', 'you
are ugly'. As an adult I am still hearing similar negative
words – 'Unfortunately you do not fit the organisation at
this time', 'you are not what we are looking for', 'you are not
satisfying enough'.

Even in the church environment I have heard – 'you are
too aggressive', 'you are too loud', 'you are too happy', 'you talk
too much'. Whilst I cannot stop what is being said about me
directly or behind my back, I can certainly control what I say
about myself. Though I must admit these words would hurt
at the time, it is not beneficial for me to repeat some of these
to myself. Doing that means, I will not be able to get them out
of my head; it means I believe what is being said about me.

This should not be the case. You have to understand,
your mouth is also an opening into your spirit. So, what
comes out of it is very crucial, whether it is words spoken to
God, to others or to yourself.

Jesus gave an analogy, which supports the notion that
indeed "you are what you say." When the religious leaders
complained His disciples were eating with unwashed hands,

Jesus replied, it's not what you eat that corrupts you, but the words that come out of your mouth. Why? Because there is a direct line from your mouth to your heart. Jesus explained:

> "Anything you eat passes through the stomach and then goes into the sewer. But the words you speak come from the heart that's what defiles you."
>
> *(Matthew 15:17-18 NLT)*

Speak life not pride

Speaking positively about yourself to others and to yourself should not result in pride or arrogance if you understand the concept very well. You do not have to speak negative about others in order to have positive things to say about yourself, or to feel good about yourself. For example, 'I am glad I am not like XYZ, who is always so depressed and miserable, I am bold and know what I want'.

You may feel like you are stating the obvious and in most cases you may be right in your 'observation'; just exercise some reservation and consideration for others. You don't have to highlight the weakness in others in order to highlight the strength in yourself.

They can be mutually exclusive, it is possible to recognise the struggles of others in humility whilst thanking God for the strength you have, also in humility. For example, this statement is less harsh and judgemental:

> "Thank God for the boldness and the ability to know what I want in life, I pray that XYZ finds that same boldness to press on."

Quick action time

Give examples of how you would speak positively about yourself without damaging others.

The main objective of watching what you say and then saying constructive, productive words to yourself, is so, it can help you to recover from rejection. It can also turn the negative effect of being rejected to a positive thing or at least reduce the effect of the rejection.

You may have had an engagement called off and the person went on to marry someone else; you may feel rejected because of your looks, possessions, education, spirituality or other factors.

Speaking positively over your life will help to alleviate low self-esteem. Confess God's Words over your life, such as:

- 'I am beautiful.'
- 'I am a blessing.'
- 'I am an overcomer.'
- 'This too shall pass'

These and many more positive words can create a positive, winning vibe for you and others.

Speak truth not lies

Honesty is indeed the best policy. In order to truly heal from rejection do not be in denial. There is no point confessing positive words if you have a negative reality, which calls for change. You may be beautiful alright, but you may have been rejected because of your attitude. So, in this instance you have to accept you have work to do, confess the change in to your life then do it. Do what you have confessed you will do.

Dear reader, I encourage you to have an attitude of expectancy, a '**can do**' attitude, then speak confidently believing in your own ability to back up your words.

Make the choice to incorporate assertive, proactive things into your life by speaking them over your life. Be careful not to rush into saying something when you don't feel it in your heart or you know it to not be true in your mind. The reason for personal rejection and disappointment in ourselves is when we say what we don't live up to. At school, in the workplace and in your personal relationships, people will hold you accountable for your words.

The tongue is a powerful member of the body; and like God, we are able to 'create our world' through our words. But remember, God is not like man. He will do precisely what He says He will do:

> "He is not a man that He should lie, and neither is He
> the son of man that He should repent."
>
> *(Numbers 23:19)*

Be a person of your word. You will be able to say things with confidence, which will yield results because you will be speaking the truth in humility.

What you say will become what you do. We end up looking like our words. A person who speaks arrogantly will 'look' arrogant and when arrogance meets exaggeration of the truth, you become an arrogant and deceived liar.

As long as you are operating with logic, reason and faith, you'll follow through and win the respect of others and most importantly, gain self-respect in the process.

I noticed sometimes, when I would repeat certain negative words spoken about me by several people, I would feel my heart breaking and I would want to 'cower somewhere' and feel the rejection all over again. This is because there is an argument in my head about whether what was said about me was true and I should really go and hide. Therefore, it is true, you have the potential to be your own worst enemy. That's why it is really important to surround yourself with things, which promote positive thinking, speaking and actions.

As a matter of fact, if you want to know what is in your heart, think about what you said today. Did your words nourish and encourage others or yourself? Were they kind?

"like honey – sweet to the soul and healthy for the body"?
(Proverbs 16:24)

James said we can tell what we're really like by the way we talk to and about others. We know better than to curse God in the presence of others, but do we curse 'those who have been made in the image of God'? If we do, then our hearts have become a 'salty spring' producing only 'bitter water.' (James 3:9-12) Even more damaging is when the bitter water in your life is produced by your own words.

Matthew Budd, MD, an assistant professor at Harvard Medical School for 20 years before retiring, was the architect for the first Behavioural Medicine department at the Harvard Community Health Plan. He co-authored a book called '*You Are What You Say*' in which he presents the principles of a powerful, scientifically validated programme, which weaves ancient and modern insights into human behaviour, neurophysiology, language, and spirituality. The underlying principle of the book is, though your words help to reflect your health and well-being, they play a major role in determining your health and state of well-being. Your words contribute to your overall wellness. He explains how the body 'learns' many of its reactions, consciously and unconsciously, through language.[1]

Budd, a medical doctor, felt he was ineffective as a doctor, unable to help most of his patients with their everyday health problems and was looking for new answers. He was convinced by a friend to attend an Erhard Seminars Training EST in search for some answers. Reluctantly he attended the seminar even though he kept his reservations about the seminar being a joke. At the seminar, a woman started to ask a question angrily, and then suffered a severe asthma attack to the point where she couldn't breathe. Thinking as a medical doctor coming to her rescue, he ran towards her, looking to intervene to rescue her from her plight. The seminar leader waved him off, and turned to the woman, and said "Look at me, I am not your father!" He asked her to look at his right ear, his nose, his mouth, and asked if those were her father's right ear, nose, mouth, and being irritated she said no. Then he said "I'm not your father, am I? So why are you so angry?" and she broke down in tears, and the asthma attack was over. Budd was stunned.

He writes of how his view on the world changed, he had learnt, words can have the effect of causing the cessation of an asthma attack, which is a physical condition. He had always held the view, such a physical ailment like an asthma attack required a physical intervention by him as a doctor, and yet the seminar leader had cleared up the attack through just words.

In his book, he went on to describe his subsequent journey in discovering how deeply intertwined our physical and mental states are. Budd details how he learned, the structure of our brain and body determine how we respond to events. Interestingly he suggests, our brains and bodies have been shaped both by our genetic inheritance, but also by all of the events we have experienced. Hence what we experience and perceive is determined by these structures, and therefore is not merely a function of what happens to us, but also our entire history. Once we accept this world view, we can no longer blame others or our situation for our responses. It's about controlling what you say, which in turn determines your reaction to situations, and ultimately shapes your destiny.

From Budd's experience we learn firstly the power of words to heal. The Bible states, *"He sent His Word and healed them and delivered them from their destructions."* (Psalm 107:2)

Secondly, the right words channelled in the right way and at the right time can expose hidden anger, bitterness and the root cause of rejection so it can be dealt with. This is something even the most skilled physician cannot diagnose or cure with just medicine for the body.

Finally, he summarises his discoveries into three A's:

Awareness: Get to know yourself. Analyse your emotions, mood and posture. Be aware of your state of mind by listening to yourself, listen to your body.

Acceptance: Understand that accepting things as it is does not mean you approve of it. Learn to separate what 'is' from what 'should be'

Action: To be consistent with a new mindset it has to be backed by actions. Consistency in aligning your current values with your actions will help produce the results you are looking for.

There is a lot of effort required to turn rejection into an agent of success. The efforts may be difficult and long drawn out, it is perfectly normal to feel the need to 'settle' when tired. Just 'see' there are better days ahead. Take little steps to victory. One confession at a time. Do you think your words match up with your actions?

Do some self-analysis and think about what you put out to the world. You'll find, what you speak over your life will become your reality if you're willing to align your words with some productive action.

Call to Action

Try some self-analysis – what are you really sad about? What is really the cause of your anger?

Below are some positive confessions you can say over your life. Remember to say it till you mean it. Some people fake it, you can 'faith' it. Say it loud enough for your ears to hear, then your heart will catch on and you will begin to act on it thereby changing your destiny:

- My status is changing.
- I can do it, I'll try.
- I am wonderfully and fearfully made by God.
- God is with me in this.
- It's not too late to try.
- It is not over for me yet.
- I have breath so I have hope
- God is bigger than my problems.

I pray, as you speak positive words over your life and your situation, you will begin to see miracles and a turnaround in your life, in Jesus' Name, Amen.

Endnotes

1: Mahew Budd, M.D. and Larry Rothstein "You Are What You Say" www.penguinrandomhouse.com/ books/20847/you-are-what-you-say-by-mahew-buddmd-and-larry-rothstein-edd/9780812929621/ (accessed May 05, 2019).

Chapter 11

Courage or Compromise

It takes courage to decide, the rejection you face can be used as an agent of success. Sometimes it takes courage to compromise on a high moral ground of seeking revenge for the wrong done to you. On the flip side it is not courageous to compromise on your beliefs and faith.

Courage is the ability to control fear and to be willing to deal with something dangerous, difficult, or unpleasant. It is defined also as an act of bravery and strength in the face of pain or grief.

It surely takes courage to face your offenders or face your fears. It is sometimes difficult and frightening to want more out of life when people have constantly told you, you are not good enough. Trying again after failing, getting up again after falling, and doing something out of the ordinary all takes courage. I commend those who do something courageous everyday no matter how little or insignificant it may seem.

When a person is going through some hard times, the last thing on their mind is to be courageous. But, just by ploughing through the day and doing the little day to day chores, you show yourself and the world what courage looks like. You do not have to put on the 'look' of bravery – whatever that is – neither do you have to assume the 'title' of courageous before you can actually *be* courageous, or before you can recognise, you *are* being brave.

I remember when I was going through the 'eye of the storm' – an extremely low point in my life. I did not want to do anything at all, all the energy was drained out of me, I had no passion for anything and no zest for life. I Just wanted to curl up somewhere dark and nurse my broken heart. It took tremendous effort to get out of bed each day for work, church, etc. It took massive effort to restrain myself from lashing out at anyone who asked me whether I was ok. It felt like torture to be kind or at least act cordially with the people who caused me pain. But I did it, every chance I got, I did it. Painful as it was, I did it. I did all I could to keep going.

It was later, I realised I was facing depression and my 'efforts' were actually acts of courage. You see it was key for me to make these 'efforts' and brave the shame to reach the shine. I would be the sore loser if I let myself cower in self-pity and regret, and nurse my broken heart. It took bravery to let God heal my heart and let Him take vengeance and vindicate me, no matter how long it takes, if at all it comes.

I do not see myself as some heroine or super woman; however, I am what I am by the grace of God. It took a while to get here but I am here anyway. The journey to becoming who God wants you to be and who you want to be is a long and lonely one. Recognising where things have gone wrong along the way is crucial for midlife correction.

You do not have to face rejection to re-evaluate your life and the steps you are taking to your destiny. Be courageous, don't just think about being brave. Be brave, just do it.

It's easier said than done sometimes, I agree. Courage is something everybody wants. It is an attribute of good character that makes us worthy of respect. We have heard of inspiring tales of courage all through history such as Esther fighting for the lives of her people, David fighting Goliath to rescue his people, and Rosa Parks who sat on the bus to defy racism. And many more like Nelson Mandela, Martin Luther King Jr.

You and I can join this list of bravery in our own little way every day by:

Choosing to Act in the Face of Fear

Courage will never be courage without fear. The presence of fear is not the absence of courage, it is the catalyst for courage. When you're afraid either to try something new or face your insecurities, you are presented with the opportunity to be courageous. This is the reason why there is no more 'perfect' time to be brave than the present. When you have to wait till you no longer 'feel' afraid, then it is not courage. After being rejected in a relationship you can easily become afraid to try another relationship or trust again because of the 'fear' of being rejected again or being hurt. Be courageous and try again, do not let fear hold you hostage to your past. There will always be the risk of being hurt or rejected. It is the reality we have to accept.

Therefore, have the courage to act now and face the fear rather than to react to fear in a cowardly way. Conquer fear by confronting it, that way it loses its hold on you even if it is present.

Following Your Heart

It is courageous to follow your heart despite it being broken through rejections. I will also advise, you follow your heart with your head in the right place. The heart is the 'centre' of emotions in simple terms. When you have carefully analysed yourself to discover what you really want with all your heart; It takes courage to be led by the heart whilst keeping your head. This is because many people simply follow the heart through emotions. Emotions can be very misleading if not harnessed and controlled. So, when following your heart, be brave enough to explore your motives honestly. Be brave to face the challenges following your heart might bring.

Persevering in the Face of Adversity

"A hero is no braver than an ordinary man, but he is braver five minutes longer."

Ralph Waldo Emerson (1803–1882)

We have to learn to face our fears in order to be courageous. We can remain courageous every day by persevering. Do not relax your efforts today because yesterday was a success. Yesterdays' struggles were for yesterday. Today presents a fresh need for courage.

The end of the hardship may not necessarily be in sight but be unrelenting in your efforts to overcome.

Learn to compartmentalise or break down challenges or a particular difficulty into smaller, conquerable challenges to overcome each day.

"Therefore, do not worry about tomorrow, for tomorrow will worry about its own things. Sufficient for the day is its own trouble."

(Matthew 6:34)

For example, I decided to get rid of everything that reminded me of the rejection I've been through. Starting from certain objects in my house. I recognised it was a mammoth task that will cost me money, time and energy. Therefore, by working on one area at a time and being patient with the rate of progress I was making, it became a lot easier to handle the pressure and juggle a lot of things at the same time.

Changing unhelpful thinking patterns: Out with the old, in with the new.

"Man cannot discover new oceans unless he has the courage to lose sight of the shore."

Andre Gide.[1]

Be determined to analyse your thought patterns. *"For as he thinks in his heart, so is he…"* (Proverbs 23:7) There are familiar thoughts, which are destructive and unhelpful. Recognising this is very important to the process of turning rejection into an agent of success.

Always thinking you are not loved by anyone is destructive and self damning. It will shrink your courage which is needed to expand your horizons or break out of your comfort zone.

You cannot discover new strengths if you are always holding on to familiar weaknesses. Today I encourage you to push harder, let go of the familiar, expand your horizon and become the courageous person you were created to be.

Embracing Suffering with Dignity and Faith

"The ideal man bears the accidents of life with dignity and grace, making the best of circumstances."

Aristotle.

"A man of courage is also full of faith."

Marcus Tullius Cicero.[2]

One of the attributes of the Almighty God is that He is Long-suffering. His name has become a swear word or a word to express disgust or exasperation. He is insulted and mocked all the time every time in world by the very people He created. He is taken for granted, unappreciated and often blamed for every bad thing that happens on the planet as an 'act of God'. Even the miracles He performs are not accredited to Him but written down as 'coincidence', 'science at its best', 'human ingenuity' and so on. He sent His Son, to the earth for the sole purpose of redeeming/ reconciling us to Himself. But He was murdered in hatred and suffered the most inhumane treatment, which could be received by anyone.

Even Satan does not appear to have 'suffered' as much as Jesus has, at least not yet. God is longsuffering, in that He is still exercising patience with us as we continue to disobey Him and disregard Him in our lives. Our very existence depends on God not losing His temper, reacting too quickly or overreacting. He patiently and faithfully continues to serve us and provide for us despite our daily betrayal.

> "But You, O Lord, are a God full of compassion,
> and gracious, longsuffering and abundant in mercy
> and truth."
>
> *(Psalms 86:15).*

Likewise, we must also brace ourselves to suffer long with dignity and faith. Just because you are in the right does not mean breakthrough will come immediately. It may take a while. It may take a while to find love again after a broken heart. The suffering of lack or loneliness may be for a while yet but stand firm each day having faith in Gods' ability to help you overcome and not in your own strength alone.

We often find it difficult to overcome rejection or go through the healing process properly because we are in a hurry to 'feel good'. The need for immediate gratification and vindication often lead to compromise on integrity and dignity. This usually leads to even more mistakes and more rejection, a ripple effect of rejection will then continue to damage the soul and destiny.

Understand, the presence of God in your life does not necessarily mean exclusion from suffering. If Jesus could endure suffering in this life, why should we be any different?

In fact, scripture advises us that if we do not partake of Jesus' suffering, we have no part in His victory.

> "Beloved, do not think it strange concerning the fiery trial which is to try you, as though some strange thing happened to you; but rejoice to the extent that you partake of Christ's sufferings, that when His glory is revealed, you may also be glad with exceeding joy. If partake of Christ's sufferings, that when His glory is revealed, you may also be glad with exceeding joy. If you are reproached for the name of Christ, blessed are you, for the Spirit of glory and of God rests upon you. On their part He is blasphemed, but on your part He is glorified. 15 But let none of you suffer as a murderer, a thief, an evildoer, or as a busybody in other people's matters. Yet if anyone suffers as a Christian, let him not be ashamed, but let him glorify God in this matter."
>
> *(1 Peter 4:12-16)*

Therefore, be courageous by enduring the pain of suffering without compromising on your dignity or your faith. You *"... can do all things through Christ that strengths you" (Philippians 4:13)*. 'all things' includes suffering for a long time. But we must take heart because:

> "... the Lord will not cast off forever. Though He causes grief, Yet He will show compassion according to the multitude of His mercies. For He does not afflict willingly, nor grieve the children of men."
>
> *(Lamentations 3:31-33)*

We must also take heart in knowing:

> "… His anger is but for a moment, His favour is for life;
> weeping may endure for a night, but joy comes in the
> morning."
>
> *(Psalm 30:5-7)*

Willingness to change without compromising

A compromise is a situation in which people accept something slightly different from what they really want, because of circumstances or because they are considering the wishes of other people.

At times we come between a rock and a hard place. This is perhaps when you have in your mind an idea of where you ought to be at this stage in your life but circumstances are dictating otherwise. Should you be resilient and unrelenting? Or should you recognise when to compromise on that particular idea and approach it in a different way.

When I realised my previous employers were looking for grounds to release me from my contract prematurely, I knew if I stayed, I may end up leaving with nothing so I decided to compromise my personal motto – 'I am a winner not a quitter' on that occasion. I prayed to God for wisdom, so I left the company with my dignity intact, I 'agreed' to quit on favourable terms.

Dear reader, recognise when it is ok to 'quit whilst winning'. Pick your battles, learn when it is necessary to stand and be courageous and be aware of when to compromise respectfully. It does not mean giving up on your dreams. It just means your dreams may need more time to be realised or you need more time to grow into your dreams.

Whatever you do, do not compromise on the fibre of who you are, your essence or your faith. Do not compromise on who and what God had called you to be. It takes courage to stay true to yourself despite any challenges. Aspire to be the best. Be the best **you**, always. With God you can do it.

Call to Action

Think of a situation as an adult when you felt afraid, yet chose to face your fear.

Now, come up with your own definition of courage, which is most meaningful to you.

What did you observe, think, and feel at the time? for example, "*I stood in front of the crowd and felt butterflies in my stomach.*"

What did you or the people around you say, think, and do to help you face your fear? For example, "*I told myself that if little kids could go on it, so could I.*"

At what point did your fear start to go down? How did you feel afterwards?

Finally, think of a situation you are currently facing, which creates fear or anxiety. What are you most afraid of? For example, being fired or not getting a raise if I speak the truth.

What mental or environmental barriers stand in the way of overcoming the fear? How can you cope with or get rid of these barriers? What/Who is your source of inspiration?

Remind yourself, you have the necessary skills to overcome as you have used them successfully in the past.

Repeat this exercise as often and as honestly as you can.

Consider how you will apply courage to these situations should they arise in the future.

Endnotes

1: Natpacker, "Man cannot discover new oceans unless …" natpacker.com/man-cannot-discover-new-oceansunless/ (accessed May 20, 2019).

2: Brainy quotes, 'Marcus Tullius Cicero Quotes www. brainyquote.com /quotes/ marcus_tullius_cicero_156290 (accessed May 20, 2019).

Chapter 12

God Of A Second Chance?

Technically, He is not. If God was only giving us second chances, then we will all have perished by now and be completely hopeless. He is rather a God of 'another' chance, but I suppose it sounds better to say 'God of a second chance'. Truth is, He keeps giving us another 'go' at making things right and re-aligning ourselves to His Word.

After experiencing rejection repeatedly, you may be tempted never to 'try' in case you get rejected again. Then you kick yourself for allowing yourself to feel the same way again. The cycle of torture continues. However, because God does not just give us second chances but lots of chances, we must also keep giving ourselves 'another chance'. Try not to be too hard on yourself. Have a go again until your pain threshold increases, and you learn to use it for your good.

I recall vividly how I blamed myself for being rejected. It was so profound, I did not feel I deserved another chance at being 'normal' or even happy. I felt my 'innocence' and blissfulness were gone out of my marriage. Never again would I feel content in my home, I felt that chance was gone. God gave us another chance. In fact, there were many other times I felt like quitting, but He kept giving us another chance to try harder, love stronger, trust harder and live happier. What an awesome God.

This is a daily chance and grace given to all His children. It is also yours for the taking. You may feel you have lost your chance at happiness because your actions led you to being rejected and so you tell yourself, you 'deserve' whatever happens to you. This is self-condemnation. Why check yourself out of the race that's barely begun? Yes, you have to admit your mistakes, but failing to learn from it and move on is tantamount to handing down your own judgement.

To be given a 'second chance' in that sense is being given a new lease of life. Sometimes the difficulties and the challenges we face act as a much needed 'break' to stop and re-evaluate the direction of your life. If you had not been released and rejected from that Job, you may have carried on mindlessly in a dead-end job. When you left, it gave you a much-needed re-balancing to determine what you really want out of life. You could even see it, the rejection you faced gave you another chance to rebase, to refresh, to love again, to explore new things, to be different, to be yourself, to free yourself from the norm or boring routines, to change yourself for you not for others as such, to be free to change your mind, change your look for you, to love your look the way you are, to love your life just as God gave you.

You will be surprised, some wish they are given a 'catalyst' for change – something to break the mould. Not everyone is bold enough to purposely instigate a 'disruption' in the routine of life. Therefore, to an extent, rejection can be expected and almost welcomed as the 'cue' to do something different or work harder.

There is clear evidence of the longing of so many for a fresh start. Yet not many actually take the leap of faith after making a mess of life, when in fact our God generously gives us countless chances to turn back to Him and enjoy His love again. God doesn't just give us a 'second chance' in life – He comes to us and transforms us into our real life. He is indeed the God of the second chance, and third chance and fourth, and fifth, sixth (and many, many more).

Dear reader, I invite you to make full use of God's graciousness and maximise the chances you have been given over and over again. Here are few suggestions on how to do it:

Decide to Make a Fresh Start

The decision to start again after losing a loved one, a job, a spouse or simply to start life over again is hard but necessary. The first move to a fresh start is to decide that you want one. Then count the cost. The decision has to be yours, or else the difficulty you face whilst making a start will be unbearable. For instance, if someone decides for you to make a fresh start and you do not buy into it; you will eventually blame that person if it does not work out as expected or you will blame that person every time you encounter a problem.

You make that decision yourself and understand, it will not be an easy task. You are challenging yourself into new things and out of your comfort zone. So, think before you leap, but make that decision to leap.

> "Do not remember the former things, nor consider the things of old. Behold, I will do a new thing, now it shall spring forth; shall you not know it? I will even make a road in the wilderness and rivers in the desert."
>
> *(Isaiah 43:18-19)*

Seize a Second Chance

A good biblical example that illustrates a 'Second Chance' is the story of Jonah.

Jonah is different from all the other prophets; he is famous for 'being in the belly of the whale' because he disobeyed and 'ran away' from God.

The book starts with Jonah disobeying God, and ends with him complaining about what God has done. It appears Jonah was angry, impatient and irritable especially towards the people of Nineveh who are also God's creation. He was particularly not happy about God's instruction to preach to them, so they too could be saved. He felt God was too lenient towards a wicked nation and rather wants them to face God's judgement rather than His mercy.

God worked within and around Jonah's weaknesses to accomplish His purposes by using a whale to intercept Jonah's flight away from his assignment.

When he hit 'rock bottom', from inside the fish Jonah prayed, "*In my distress I called to the Lord ... you listened to my cry*" *(Jonah 2:2)*. Perhaps, you find yourself in unusual or difficult circumstances. No matter how desperate or hopeless your situation may seem, it is never too late.

He recognised what we miss out on when we do not follow the Lord's instructions. *"Those who cling to worthless idols forfeit the grace that could be theirs"* (Jonah 2:8).

It is so easy to put our trust in something other than God. We may not worship actual idols, but we can so often put our trust in the 'idols' of money, success, fame, sex or anything, which takes us away from God and prevents us from receiving the grace that can be ours.

Once the decision has been made to make a fresh start, seize the opportunity and do it. Always remember, *God's love will never let you down.* God's love can reach you no matter how far you've fallen.

There is no situation God cannot rescue you from if you cry out to Him.

God's Love Means You Get a Second Chance

God was persistent in giving Jonah a second chance and when Jonah took him up on it, the result was an eternal impact on many people's lives.

Then the word of the Lord came to Jonah a second time – *"Go to the great city of Nineveh and proclaim to it the message I give you"* (Jonah 3:2). This is almost exactly what God had said to him earlier (Jonah 1:2). The first time he messed up. The second time, God used him powerfully.

Not only did God give Jonah a second chance, He also gave the city of Nineveh a second chance.

Nineveh was a great city. It had more than 120,000

people. As a result of Jonah's message, the people repented; they believed. The king believed. Revival came as a result of one person's preaching, thousands were saved.

Your 'second chance' today means victory for someone else tomorrow. Someone can also benefit from your new lease of life or from your new view of life.

Therefore, be careful not to impede someone else's second chance. You may be reluctant to accept, the persons who betrayed you or rejected you have turned a new leaf and are also on a journey to living their best life. Like Jonah, this may easily bring about fresh anger and re open old wounds leading to bitterness.

Jonah's 'second chance' meant, he was given another go at fulfilling his calling. After all the success of his evangelistic campaign, he fell into another deep depression. He was angry with God. He was angry that they had repented. The Ninevites were cruel oppressors. They were into witchcraft, torture, greed and prostitution. Yet they repented and God forgave them.

Jonah, forgetting what God had saved him from was quick to anger, unlike God who has great patience, not easily angered, rich in love, and ready to apply grace and mercy at the drop of a hat to throw our sins and plans of punishment into the sea of forgiveness and forgetfulness!

This still happens today – some find it hard when evil people repent and God forgives them.

I have come to learn, giving someone a second chance means we give them another chance to earn our trust. It does not mean we instantly forget what experience has taught us. Trust must be earned over time, and we are foolish if we give trust prematurely. We can have a loving and forgiving heart, which also practices wise guardianship over our lives.

On the other hand, we must exercise patience when we have wronged someone. It will be unwise to demand another chance without allowing the aggrieved person to arrive at that decision on their own. We should work to earn another chance by continued demonstration of repentance and change.

It is understandable, there may come a time in a human relationship when second chances are no longer effective. It may be dangerous to keep giving an abusive husband 'second chances' especially if they show no commitment towards change. A clear example of this, would be if the same thing keeps re occurring – in that forgiveness has been offered and restoration made possible, but one-party refuses to repent and rejects all efforts to reconcile. It is important to recognise when it may be time to end that relationship. Ending a relationship is a last resort, but sometimes it must be done:

> "Moreover, if your brother sins against you, go and tell him his fault between you and him alone. If he hears you, you have gained your brother. But if he will not hear, take with you one or two more, that 'by the mouth of two or three witnesses every word may be established.' And if he refuses to hear them, tell it to the church. But if he refuses even to hear the church, let him be to you like a heathen and a tax collector.."
>
> *(Matthew 18:15-17)*

Likewise, God does everything possible to draw us to repentance, offering forgiveness and second chances:

> "The Lord is not slack concerning His promise, as some
> count slackness, but is longsuffering toward us, not
> willing that any should perish but that all should come
> to repentance."
>
> *(2 Peter 3:9)*

But if we continue to reject Him, the offer is withdrawn and, at death, there are no more chances.

> "What shall we say then? Shall we continue in sin,
> that grace may abound?"
>
> *(Romans 6:1)*

> "And as it is appointed for men to die once,
> but after this the judgement."
>
> *(Hebrews 9:27)*

God's grace is our model. We can offer second chances to others until a healthy relationship is no longer possible. Even then you should still keep an open policy, not necessarily to restart the broken relationship, but to offer forgiveness.

Enjoy a Radical Life Change

Wearing a new shoe looks good but often does not feel good initially. We know it gets better over time and with frequent use. Likewise, there will be some discomforts associated with a new life change. This does not mean to quit or complain about the new chance you have been given. Wear the change with a smile, even if it pinches still. It does get better with time, think about it, the new thing today is old by tomorrow. So, enjoy a radical life change. Make the best of it and always look for other opportunities to live your best life.

Note, you cannot fully enjoy your 'second chance' by dwelling on 'past chances' or 'wasted chances'. That is no way to live. Do not do it to yourself. Learn from the past, focus on the present and leave the future to God.

Do not live life looking over your shoulder or sideways to take cues from others on how to be a better you. Jesus is our ultimate example for righteousness and on how to live a 'purpose driven life'. It does not mean we cannot learn from others. Of course, we ought to learn from others, but we must learn circumspectly and wisely, considering yourself and without judging others. It is so easy to judge other people about the very things we do ourselves. We tend to look at ourselves through rose-tinted glasses and look at everyone else through a magnifying glass. A judgemental mind focuses on what is wrong with others, rather than on what is right.

> "Therefore, you are inexcusable, O man, whoever you are who judge, for in whatever you judge another you condemn yourself; for you who judge practice the same things. But we know that the judgement of God is according to truth against those who practice such things. And do you think this, O man, you who judge those practising such things, and doing the same, that you will escape the judgement of God? Or do you despise the riches of His goodness, forbearance, and longsuffering, not knowing that the goodness of God

leads you to repentance? 5 But in accordance with your
hardness and your [a]impenitent heart you are
[b]treasuring up for yourself wrath in the day of wrath
and revelation of the righteous judgement of God,
6 who "will render to each one according to his deeds."

(Romans 2:1-6)

Enjoying a radical new life also means being unencumbered by guilt of sin and shame. We have all sinned and in need of repentance:

"… for all have sinned, and come short
of the glory of God."

(Romans 3:23)

Giving yourself another chance means to forgive yourself and others. God's kindness is intended to lead us to repentance. The moment we repent and turn to God, we get a second chance, the possibility of a new life. The Bible is full of people who received second chances, and even third and fourth chances. Prominent examples of God's grace may be seen in the lives of Peter, Jonah, Mark, Samson, David, and others.

The psalmist states it well:

"… but you, O Lord, are a God merciful and gracious,
slow to anger and abounding in steadfast love and
faithfulness."

(Psalm 86:15)

The prophet Micah praises God:

"Who is a God like you, pardoning iniquity and passing over transgression for the remnant of his inheritance? He does not retain his anger forever, because he delights in steadfast love."

(Micah 7:18)

Prayer:

Lord, forgive me for the times when I judge others for the very things that I do myself. Thank You for the riches of your kindness, love and forgiveness made possible through the blood of Jesus Christ. Thank You that every day is an opportunity for a new start – a second chance.

Lord, thank You for Your great love. Thank You that even when I have messed up, You give me a second chance. Help me to bring the good news of Your love to others so that they too may turn back to your love.

Amen.

Afterword

Looking Beyond

I am not completely sure of what God has in store for me and my marriage but I am completely sure of His Word and His thoughts of good towards my husband and me.

Dear reader, please understand, success is relative. What I deem to be success may not be what you deem to be success. For everything I have been through in my life, it became important for me to be able to define and redefine what 'success' is to *me*.

What does success look like for me? What does 'happiness' mean for me? I have often thought about it and it has made me honest and frank with myself.

The obvious success would be to tell you that my marriage is back on track and fully functioning, that everything is going well and 'life is gravy again'. Another obvious success perhaps would be for me to state here that my marriage is annulled due to unfaithfulness and that I have now found 'closure'.

No, my success is none of that. I am still seeking the Will of God my Father as to what steps to take. I do not take lightly the consequences of my actions in whatever I decide to do.

I will say, this book is written for people who have not got it all figured out and have won the battle against rejection. It is for people to be able to see, there can be 'success' in pain, in sorrow, in rejection, in sickness, indeed in various forms despite the challenges they face every day and in every way.

I count my blessings; I consciously name the little victories I see one by one, and I am always amazed at what God is doing in my life. I am determined to enjoy God's daily mercies and grace.

My faith in God is still resolute despite the storm, the grace and ability to write and publish my story in this book, the boldness to confront my insecurities, the grace to live and thrive in the presence of my enemies, my zest for life, my appetite for greatness are all part of what I call 'my success'.

In conclusion, I do not claim to have all that I want in this life. I do not claim to have attained the 'height' of success as many have. Neither do I claim to have what you would class as success; what I do know is that I have not and will not let rejection make me refrain from living, thriving and being the best God wants me to be.

As apostle Paul states:

"Brothers and sisters, I do not consider myself yet to have taken hold of it. But one thing I do: Forgetting what is behind and straining toward what is ahead, I press on toward the goal to win the prize for which God has called me heavenward in Christ Jesus."

(Philippians 3:13-14)

One area of your life may not be going as planned but it does not mean you cannot achieve success in life.

Be bold to accept the hand life has dealt you, and then strive to achieve success with it.

Regardless of the outcome of your situation, you will always have a place in the Father's heart, and you are "... *accepted in the Beloved." (Ephesians 1:6)*

Be clear of what success means to you, not just what others think it should be.

Remember to use God's Word as your guide, seek counsel wisely. Ultimately, the power to make **Rejection an Agent of Success** is in you!

Also by the Author

In *The Art of Making Music to God's Glory*, the author shares some best practices she has learnt as a choir director. It offers both spiritual and practical insights into making music to the glory of God. She currently holds choir/worship workshops using her book as a point of reference.